High Yello Rose
and Other Texas Plays

Sterling Houston
1945 – 2006

High Yello Rose
and Other Texas Plays

by Sterling Houston

Edited, with Introduction and Notes by

Sandra M. Mayo, Ph.D.

WingsPress

San Antonio, Texas
2009

Cover photo: Jump-Start Performance Company, production of
High Yello Rose. Left to Right: Katherine Griffith, Kim Corbin, Veronica Gonzales

First Edition
ISBN: 978-0-916727-54-3

Wings Press
627 E. Guenther • San Antonio, Texas 78210
Phone/fax: (210) 271-7805

On-line catalogue and ordering:
www.wingspress.com
All Wings Press titles are distributed to the trade by
Independent Publishers Group • www.ipgbook.com

This publication is made possible in part by a generous grant from
the City of San Antonio, Department of Cultural Affairs.

Library of Congress Cataloging-in-Publication Data:

Houston, Sterling, 1945-
  High yello rose : and other Texas plays / by Sterling Houston ; edited,
with introduction and notes by Sandra M. Mayo. -- 1st ed.
    p. cm.
  ISBN 978-0-916727-54-3 (alk. paper)
  1. Texas--Drama. I. Title.
  PS3608.O875H54 2009
  812'.6--dc22   2009005129

Contents

Photographs

The Myth of History
An Introduction

Sandra Mayo, Ph.D.

Most of what I do is historically based. It has some grounding in history or myth. I don't differentiate much between the two. History is mythology; mythology is history in a way of thinking.[1]

– Sterling Houston

Sterling Houston (1945-2006) was born in San Antonio, Texas. He graduated from Highlands High School in 1963. After working on both the East and West Coasts as a performer and writer, he returned to San Antonio as an experienced theatre professional and found his calling and voice in playwriting. In his outpouring of 33 plays written from 1988 to 2006 he frequently turned for inspiration to what he said he knew best, Texas—especially San Antonio and its historically African American East Side.

Sterling Houston's canon includes 13 historical plays; seven with the Texas milieu as the focal point. They highlight his lifetime, but also go back over 100 years to the fight for Texas and the early years of the 19th and 20th century in the Alamo City. *High Yello Rose* takes us back to 1835-36 in the midst of the salient events of the Texas Revolution. *Living Graves* starts in the early years of the 21st century but reflects back to the early 1800s in developing San Antonio. *Miss Bowden's Dream* starts at the turn of the century in 1902 when Miss Artemesia Bowden began academic leadership of St. Philip's Episcopal School and moves forward in time to the 1940s when St. Philip's joins the Alamo Community College District. *Cameoland* and *Driving Wheel* turn to the post-world war years of the 1940s, while *Black Lily and White Lily* highlights the pre-civil rights era of the

1950s. *La Frontera* brings to the fore the post-segregation, post civil rights era of the 1990s.

Houston dramatizes the story of Emily West Morgan in *High Yello Rose* from the point of the view of the African Americans usually forgotten in most books, films, and plays. Houston grew up in the shadow of the Alamo and like all Texas students learned about the great legends of the Alamo—Colonels Jim Bowie, Davy Crockett, and William Travis, Generals Sam Houston and Santa Anna. Emily, a mulatto bondwoman (indentured servant) and Joe, composite of several slaves or indentured servants that were connected with the legend, are the central characters in Sterling Houston's drama.

Emily West/Morgan takes the stage in *High Yello Rose* as a player on the historic stage. Houston takes his story from the various accounts, whether fact or fiction, that Emily was with Santa Anna, in his tent distracting him, when he was defeated at San Jacinto. Although the legendary stories and historical notes vary, in Houston's interpretation Emily is in Santa Anna's tent by choice in a conscious effort to distract him while Joe leads General Sam Houston to the location. Also in Houston's comedy, Joe and Emily are separated after the war and Joe writes a tribute to her in song, the song we know as the "Yellow Rose of Texas."

Historical records document that Emily was under a labor contract with James Morgan of Galveston Bay and was among the captives of the Mexican Army at his home site who were transported to the San Jacinto battle site. Census records suggest that she was a free black in New Haven, Connecticut, prior to signing an indentured servant contract with James Morgan. Campfire and barroom tales after the battle state that Santa Anna was with her, caught with his pants down, when attacked and defeated by General Houston.[2] The most cited evidence of this comes from the journal of a visiting English traveler, William Bollaert. Journalists and historians embellished the account, including Frank X. Tolbert in *The Day of San Jacinto* (1959) and Ralph Henderson Shuffler, publicist for Texas A & M University in the 1950s, writing in the *Southwestern Historical Quarterly*. Shuffler, in speeches made at the Harry Ranson Humanities Research Center at the University of Texas in the 1960s, also suggested that Emily was the fitting candidate for the identity of the girl in the then-popular Mitch Miller version of "The Yellow Rose of Texas." In 1976 Martha Anne Turner, a professor at Sam Houston State University, published a small book entitled *The Yellow Rose of Texas and Her Song,* adding to the historical accounts.

The manuscript of a poem, not music, surfaced around 1836. The writer was identified as black because of the following lyrics:

> There's a yellow rose in Texas
> That I am going to see
> No other darky knows her
> No one only me
>
> She cryed so when I left her
> It like to broke my heart
> And if I ever find her
> We nevermore will part
>
> She's the sweetest rose of color
> This darky ever knew
> Her eyes are bright as diamonds
> They sparkle like the dew
>
> You may talk about dearest May
> And sing of Rosa Lee
> But the yellow rose of Texas
> Beats the belles of Tennessee [3]

The writer is obviously an African American Texian, possibly a soldier or runaway slave. John Davis notes that by the Civil War the words had found music and the lyrics were altered to avoid reference to blacks.[4] In 1936 David W. Guion developed a concert arrangement for the Texas Centennial (dedicated to Franklin D. Roosevelt, who ordered a White House performance), and in 1955 Mitch Miller recorded an arrangement for Columbia Records. The lyrics were altered as follows:

> She's the sweetest little rosebud,
> That Texas ever knew
> Her eyes are bright as diamonds,
> They sparkle like the dew,

You may talk about your Clementine
And sing of Rosalee,
But The Yellow Rose of Texas
Is the only girl for me! [5]

In *High Yello Rose,* with great irreverence, Houston caricatures the larger-than-life legendary figures of the revolution. "The eight-member, all-female cast roars into the script with the fury of wild mustangs. . . . They mug it up to great effect, mocking the Lone Star legend with a dose of high melodrama that defuses bitterness and keeps it fun." [6]

William Martin, in his analysis of Ramsey Yelvington's play on the Alamo, *A Cloud of Witnesses,* in *Texas Plays,* says,

> The legendary hold that the Battle of the Alamo has on Texans' imaginations foredooms a modern stage version to one or another kind of failure. If the playwright treats the subject with awe, the work is likely to be dismissed as one-dimensional pageantry and hero worship. If the playwright deviates from the familiar version, the work can be labeled as revisionist and considered damaging to Texans' respect for their heroic past. [7]

Yelvington's *A Cloud of Witnesses* leans toward pageantry and awe; Houston's *High Yello Rose* is without a doubt the latter—revisionist, but without arousing the expected rancor and hard feelings. Both plays have received numerous productions and accolades.

In 2004, Houston received a commission to participate in a project focused on the history of City Cemetery No. 1, located on San Antonio's East Side. This long neglected site houses the tombs, graves, and mausoleums of thousands of citizens, both prominent and obscure, who were actors in the diverse history of the thriving metropolis. With the docudrama *Living Graves: Stories from the Powder Hill Cemeteries,* Houston brings historical figures back from the other side to tell their stories, including Samuel A. Maverick, vaudeville theatre owner and gambler Jack Harris, Clara Driscoll, and her archrival Adina DeZavala. The characters support and refute each other as they reminisce in monologues, action scenes, and songs. Samuel Maverick adds humor by complaining about the attention to the battle between

Adina de Zavala and Clara Driscoll over the Alamo's legacy:

> Am I confused, misinformed, or downright delusional!? I could'a swore that this first section was mine to tell of me and the progeny that my esteemed family has produced through the generations, but instead. . . . Here we go again jawing about the Alamo. [8]

Houston takes larger-than-life historical characters and personalizes their stories so we feel we know them. For example, Samuel Maverick (1803-1870) was a Texas lawyer, politician, and cattle baron. He was caught up in the Texas Revolution, mayor of San Antonio for a while, member of the Texas legislature, and owner of over 300,000 acres of West Texas land when he died. But Houston highlights the human side—his fight against secession and for an end to slavery, his grief over a lost child, and skirmishes with Comanches. Speaking of his many battles, Maverick says in *Living Graves:*

> Is it not enough that I have had to fight off Comanches, thieving outlaws, General Santa Anna's army, reconstruction, carpetbaggers, the Ku Klux Klan, charlatans of every persuasion? Now I'm supposed to tolerate this spiritualist con woman who brings false hope to my long suffering wife. [9]

The Powder Hill cemeteries were not open to African American burial; therefore, Houston included the ghosts of black slaves/servants as commenting on visitors—resembling a Greek chorus. In the production, the black characters were placed behind a translucent scrim. In the production program, the playwright reflects:

> My theatrical explorations of American history are always viewed through a contemporary lens. Perhaps those days were not so simple after all. Perhaps the inevitable complexity and uncertainty have been so camouflaged as to be unperceived. The actual blow-by-blow of history is of less interest to me than are the implications of our endless capacity to cope with it, and keep moving on. In the end, in time, we transform the ephemera of history into the permanence of myth.[10]

Miss Bowden's Dream spans the years from 1902 to 1942, with a brief epilogue highlighting 1968 to the present. It is not only a portrait of the indomitable spirit of Artemesia Bowden, who led St. Philip's School, later St. Philip's College, in San Antonio for 50 years, but also a snapshot of the journey of African Americans to lift themselves by their bootstraps to progress by casting down their buckets to develop practical technical skills, as Booker T. Washington suggested. St. Philip's was a "normal" and industrial school for girls in 1902, supported by the Episcopal Church, when Miss Bowden took over as a teacher and administrator. She led the school through difficult financial times, especially during the Depression, to become a junior college by 1926, and then part of the Alamo Community College District in 1942. She retired as Dean Emerita in the 1960s and died in 1968. The one-time sewing school for African American girls is now a historically Black college that is "the pride of the East Side" with a diverse faculty, staff, and student body.

In 1998 Houston made a significant contribution to St. Philip's College's centennial celebration when he accepted a commission to write a play about Miss Bowden's accomplishments. His connection to the history was uncanny. "It's a funny coincidence," he wrote. "I grew up in the house my family owned on South Walters across from the St. Philip's campus. Miss Bowden was in my consciousness since I was born. My family knew her. I met her as a kid in the '50s."[11]

With *Cameoland*, Houston had the opportunity to reflect on another part of San Antonio's East Side history. He called the work "a nostalgic fantasy drenched in blues . . . a celebration of some hidden history from San Antonio's African American community before integration."[12] The play looks at life on and around East Commerce Street between 1930 and 1960. It takes the audience back to the old Cameo Theatre built in the 1940s with a live stage for vaudeville and music acts as well as a movie screen. The work includes several clips from the 1940s movie, *The Thief of Bagdad*, juxtaposed with a collage projection of images of the area from that time period, including a shoeshine stand, a beauty shop, and the Southern Pacific train station—with accompanying train sounds.

Cameoland not only reflects on life around the railroad station, musical entertainment, beauty shops, and shoeshine stands but also throws into relief the community that involved bootleggers, gamblers, murderers, and numbers runners. In the play, everyone seems to know the story of the fictional character Straight-Eight—a scarred, knife-wielding woman who dies in prison, but not before she has a grand, well-attended funeral. Houston acknowledges that the East Side history includes the stories of many "upstanding folks"—civic leaders, doctors, teachers, lawyers, and preachers, but through a main character, Joe, he makes it clear that their stories are not central in this work. Houston is more interested in the average Joe trying to overcome the challenges of racism and poverty to find some joy in life. Because the Cameo Theatre was a place for entertainment he seems especially interested in showcasing how the community amused itself, or escaped everyday challenges, in a world of music and entertainment. Many of the entertaining musical selections speak of struggle and disappointment—though not without hope.

Jasmina Wellinghoff notes in her article "*Cameoland:* A Love Song to S.A.s Old East Side," that the stories came from many sources, including stories Houston's father told him, his own memories, and the many personal accounts he collected for an oral history project funded by the Rockefeller Foundation.[13] In typical Houston style, the work is based on fact, but replete with myth or fiction. As Houston states, "I take the facts and re-form them into a mythological form to tell a deeper truth about history. Fiction can speak about history better than bare facts. It can be more accurate about the *sense* of it."[14]

Driving Wheel: a memory play, is set in the mid-1960s, with flashbacks to earlier years. It is an autobiographical fiction based loosely on Houston's own search for closure with his father. In the play the young protagonist poet struggles with coming of age, but also with his sensitivity and his father's reaction to his homosexuality. It is one of the few works in which Houston alludes to his sexuality. In an interview with Keith Hennessy he is more explicit:

> Because of my background and my racial and sexual orientation, I have a certain view of conventional history that really affects how I interpret it and how theatrically it is presented. I would never think of myself as a gay writer or a black writer, but certainly my being gay and being black totally affect the way my work is presented and envisioned.[15]

Focusing on the social and racial issues, Edna Silva notes, "Set against the background of the Civil Rights Movement, the play chronicles the dawning awareness of Blackness in San Antonio."[16] It is a potboiler of social, racial, political issues. The last scene is a particularly poignant flashback to an early stage when mother and son were kicked out of Playland Park because they were black.

Houston says of the play, "It's about the community. There's never been a play written about the East Side of San Antonio. Never! Why not?" [17] This comment was made in 1992 when the play was written and produced, before Houston's major historical works featuring the East Side—*La Frontera* (1993), *Miss Bowden's Dream* (1998), *Cameoland* (2002), and *Living Graves* (2005). The work obviously marks a turning point in his commitment to use his art to tell the story of his community.

Houston looks at race relations in the 1950s in *Black Lily and White Lily*. In this case, there is an unequal distribution of power between the Black Lily, African American maid Lily Mae, and Lily Winslow, her wealthy white employer. African American women have always been able to find domestic work in America in the homes of middle and upper class whites. Though in the bosom of the home and intimately involved in its daily activities, the domestics were nonetheless also set apart and disrespected. Houston chronicles the uneasy relationship between employer and employee through Lily Mae and Lily Winslow as they reveal an interdependence and even love/hate relationship. Though the characters and the storyline are fictional, Houston based the situation on his own mother's history of domestic service in San Antonio. His mother was successful in realizing her goal to leave domestic service and become an entrepreneur with her own travel agency.[18] *Black Lily and White Lily* is a short piece that works well on a playbill of one or two other plays featuring race, class, and/or generation gap issues for women.

Set in the 1990s, *La Frontera*—as its title suggests—is about borders, or the lines often drawn between neighbors and races. Houston said he wanted to do something where African Americans dealt with their own prejudices, and at the same time highlight the richness of the two cultures (Mexican American and African American) and their commonalities, like the love of music.[19] In *La Frontera*, a Mexican American family moves into a middle class section of San Antonio's East Side—next to an African American family—evoking some predictable reactions on both sides along ethnic lines. All of the characters are fictional; however, the play showcases the changing history of the United States as reflected in Texas on San Antonio's East Side as integration stimulated by the 1960s civil rights movement led people to merge in once traditional homogenous neighborhoods.

Throughout these seven plays—farce, domestic tragedy, domestic magical realism, and musical docudramas—Sterling Houston becomes, as one reviewer called him, a "story teller/history teller."[20] Three of them are domestic dramas that reflect the influence of naturalism/realism—*Black Lily and White Lily*, *La Frontera*, and especially *Driving Wheel*. The body of Houston's work shows him as first and foremost a post modern avant-garde satirist influenced by the eclectic, technical pastiche, anything goes, rebellious and extravagant flare of artists working in America and abroad from the 1960s to the present.

Touches can be found in Houston's work from the East Coast influence of satirists George Wolfe, Suzan Lori Parks, Adrienne Kennedy, and Tony Kushner, as well as Charles Ludlam, Ronald Tavel, Tony Preston, and John Vaccaro, all of whom Houston encountered at the Playhouse of the Ridiculous. The Magic Theatre in San Francisco and the San Francisco Mime Troupe on the West Coast, both places where Houston worked, also influenced his way of envisioning and creating theatre.

All of the historical works in this collection, except *Black Lily and White Lily*, reflect his musical training and love of pop or rock and roll music, jazz, and blues, and the American musical commercial genre. Like playwright Sam Shepard, who Houston observed while working at the Magic Theatre in San Francisco, most of his plays have music. Both Houston and Shepard are "products" or "inventions of the sixties with a love for movies and rock and roll." Both are men with divided loyalties—musicians, actors, and writers.[21]

The West Coast's influence on Houston's aesthetic also comes from a knowledge and respect for Luiz Valdez's theatrical techniques. Valdez's skillfully combines *mitos* (myth), *actos* (agitprop/protest), and *corridos* (ballads) in his work at El Teatro Compesino—most successfully realized in his play *Zoot Suit*. Sterling Houston's work often combines the entertainment of the musical with the serious punch of social drama while lifting up community legends and myths, e.g. *Cameoland*.

Steve Bennett cogently summarizes Houston's theatricality in "The Stage is His Lab":

> Houston combines drama, music, dance, the visual arts and video, improvisational theater, performance art, comedy and satire. He is open to experimentation, keen to collaborate . . . Houston weaves disparate threads into colorful, contemporary slices of life. He attacks racial, sexual, familial and gender stereotypes by presenting various points of view and allowing the audience to make up its mind.[22]

Houston says, "I'm difficult to niche. If there is any theme to my work, it's mythology, whether it's ancient myth or urban myth."[23]

Making a Name in the Alamo City

Sterling Houston was a unique talent in San Antonio and the South. He joined Jump-Start Performance Co. in 1986 as a performer and had by 1989 become its writer-in-residence, by 1990 its administrative director, and shortly thereafter its artistic director, a position he held until his death in 2006. For over twenty years he had a productive relationship with the founder of the company, director of many of his plays, and long time executive director, and now education director, Steve Bailey. Over the years, Houston's work became the centerpiece of Jump-Start. At the time of Houston's death in 2006, the company had produced at 22 of his plays, alone or in collaboration with other theatres or organizations, including *Womandingo, Kool Jams, High Yello Rose, Isis in Nubia, Driving Wheel, Miranda Rites, La Frontera, Santo Negro,* and *Living Graves.*

Jump-Start Performance Co. was a perfect fit for Sterling Houston. From its inception Jump-Start has been an avant-garde company focused on new ideas in the arts. They have provided a consistent venue for a diverse group of artists creating work from many ethnic perspectives, as well as gay and straight, and more. It is a company of approximately 18 to 20 core artists who vary not only in ethnicity but also aesthetic approach and artistic disciplines—visual artists, videographers, actors, dancers, designers, writers, and musicians. Founded in 1985, they had produced over 500 original works by the end of the 2008-2009 season. Their season of four to six new company works has reached beyond San Antonio to tour nationally. Their outreach for almost fifteen years has included service to over 100,000 students in over 80 schools and community groups.[24]

Sterling Houston's work, as he says, "is iconographic of Jump-Start."[25] His body of work exemplifies Jump-Start's spirit of inclusiveness. He wrote most of his plays envisioning them performed by the Jump-Start multiethnic company of actors. The collaborative nature of the work at Jump-Start and the esprit de corps built by the company over the years gave Houston a forum for his ideas and the realization of them in art through a trusted and talented group of artists.

In San Antonio and across the country, Sterling Houston's admirers have been a mixture of the voiceless and the powerful. State Senator Ruth Jones McClendon of San Antonio issued a proclamation in recognition of his contributions to the arts in Texas. Maya Angelou responded with joyful tears and applause to his theatrical interpretation of her poem, *On the Pulse of Morning*. Houston revealed that even those he expected to object to his irreverent and sometimes outrageous interpretations, as in *High Yello Rose*, have applauded his fresh look, his attempt to expose lies and distortions.

Over 18 years, working from his base at JumpStart, Houston received a number of local, regional, and national awards and grants that demonstrate the appreciative response of the San Antonio community and a wider community of supporters. He is, artistically, a favorite son in the Alamo City. In 2007, Jump-Start produced *Hollywood and Time*, Houston's last play. Shortly before his death in November, 2006, Houston was honored to learn that the University of Texas at San Antonio had chosen to acquire his papers for their permanent San Antonio Authors Collection.[26] Sterling Houston found that living and working in San Antonio provided fertile ground for his artistic talent.

Notes

1. Sterling Houston, Interview with Keith Hennessy; available from http://www.community arts.net reading room/archive/perfcomm/ jumpstart/interview/jump-h; Internet. accessed 4 April 2008.

2. West, Emily, The Handbook of Texas Online; available from www. tsha.utexas.edu/handbook/online/articles/WW/fwe41.html; Internet: accessed 15 November, 2007.

3. John L. Davis, "The Yello Rose"; available at http://texancultures. com/education/TheYellowRose.htm; accessed 15 November 2007.

4. Ibid.

5. Ibid.

6. Robert Faires, review of *High Yello Rose*, in *The Austin Chronicle*, Vol. XIII, 10 September 1993.

7. William B. Martin, "Introduction," *A Cloud of Witnesses* by Ramsey Yelvington, in *Texas Plays*, (Southern Methodist University Press, 1990), 4.

8. Sterling Houston, *Living Graves*, in *High Yello Rose and Other Texas Plays*, ed. Sandra Mayo (Wings Press, 2009).

9. Ibid.

10. Sterling Houston, *The Living Graves: Stories from the Powder Hill Cemeteries*, Production Program, (San Antonio, TX: JumpStart Performance Co. and the Carver Community Cultural Center, 2005).

11. Kristina Paledes, "In Search of a Local Legend," review of *Miss Bowden's Dream*, in *San Antonio Express-News*, 13 November, 1998, 3, 5.

12. *Cameoland*, Promotional Flyer, (San Antonio, TX: JumpStart Performance Co. and the Carver Community Cultural Center, 2003).

13. Jasmina Wellinghoff, "*Cameoland* a Love Song to S.A.s Old East Side," review of *Cameoland*, in *San Antonio Express-News*, 2 February, 2003. (web posted)

14. Ibid.

15. Keith Hennessey, "Interview with Sterling Houston, artistic director, company manager, communityartsnetwork"; http://www.communityarts.net/readingroom/archive/perfcomm/jumpstart/interviews/jump-html; accessed 4 May 2008.

16. Elda Silva, "*Driving Wheel*: East Side Experiences Fuel Poignant Play," review of *Driving Wheel*, in *The San Antonio Light*, 6 May, 1992, C1.

17. Ibid.

18. Sterling Houston, interview by Sandra Mayo, "An Interview with Playwright Sterling Houston," (*Texas Theatre Journal*, Vol.3 Number 1, 2007) 30.

19. Ramiro Burr, "Plays at the Guadalupe Focus on Culture, Race Relations," *San Antonio Express-News*, Lifestyle/Arts, 3 March, 1993.

20. Elda Silva, "Storyteller, History-Teller: Houston's Words Speak Volumes," on *Cameoland*, in *San Antonio Express-News*, 27 January, 2002.

21. Bigsby, C.W.E., *Modern American Drama: 1945-1990* (Cambridge University Press, 1992.

22. Steve Bennett, "The Stage is His Lab," *San Antonio Express-News*, 17 August, 1997.

23. Ibid.

24. Sterling Houston, ed. *Jump-Start PlayWorks*, (Wings Press, 2004) 208.

25. Sterling Houston, interview by Sandra Mayo, "An Interview with Playwright Sterling Houston," (*Texas Theatre Journal*, Vol.3 Number 1, 2007).

26. The acquisition of Sterling Houston's papers by the University of Texas at San Antonio's permanent San Antonio Authors Collection was first proposed by the publisher of Wings Press. A descriptive summary catalog of the collection is available at:
    http://www.lib.utexas.edu/taro/utsa/00129/00129-P.html

High Yello Rose

Una Legeñda Verdadera de la Revolucion de Tejas

Note: As You Read *High Yello Rose* . . .

With *High Yello Rose,* historian and storyteller Sterling Houston recreates in hilarious comic style the legend of the Texas Revolution. The work is a tour de force of post modern theatricality. It is nonrealistic with its songs, direct address to the audience, and characters commenting on themselves as characters and the work as art. Its eclectic buffoonery brings to mind the historical comic tradition including the satyr plays in Ancient Greece in the 5th century B.C.E., Italian commedia stock character like the braggart soldier, cross dressing during the Elizabethan and Restoration period, and comic practices in the last 100 hundred years, especially the fun and frolicking of the 1970s Theatre of Ridiculous, led by Charles Ludlam. Houston creates a drama with events surrounding the historical battles of the Alamo and San Jacinto and the larger-than-life generals who led them--General López de Santa Anna and General Sam Houston. However, while satirizing the traditional historical figures, he moves to the center lesser known historical knowledge and legend.

Emily West/Morgan, a mulatto indentured servant, takes the stage as the inspiration behind the famous song "The Yellow Rose of Texas" and a player on the historic stage. Houston takes his story from the various accounts, whether fact or fiction, that Emily was with Santa Anna, in his tent distracting him, when he was defeated at San Jacinto. Although the legends and historical notes vary, Houston puts her in Santa Anna's tent by choice to help the Texians defeat the Mexicans. In *High Yello Rose,* Joe, a former slave and/or black Texian soldier, thirty years after the famous events of the Texas Revolution, finds Emily, the love of his life, who was lost to him after the revolution, and they reminisce about their involvement—this is the core of the drama. Over two acts and a total of 14 scenes Emily and Joe are placed in the midst of historical events as active change agents.

Houston caricatures Sam Houston, Santa Anna, Davy Crockett, and other Texians involved in the struggle with an all-female cast playing all the parts. Casting the heroic males with women gave Houston a certain amount of freedom and flexibility to portray the male characters' as vicious, egotistical, macho, libido-driven braggart warriors. The impersonation creates a distance that encourages the audience to think critically and differently about the famous historical events and characters.

Production Notes:

High Yello Rose was first presented by JumpStart Performance Co. on April 27, 1992 with the following cast:

Joe John Joshua	Gertrude E. Baker
Eastern Lady, Texian Soldier Col. Morgan, Old Anglo Woman	Deborah Basham
Emily Morgan, David Crockett	Kim Corbin
Magdalena, Santanista Soldier	Felice Garcia
General Santa Anna	Veronica Gonzales
General Sam Houston	Katherine Griffith
Eastern Lady, Texian Soldier	Cathleen Pollock
Conception, Miguelito, Santanista Soldier	Lisa Suarez

Directed by Arnold Aprill and Sterling Houston
Production Design by Robert Rehm
Lighting Design by Max Parrilla
Written in collaboration with Arnold Aprill

High Yello Rose was presented in the fall of 1993 with the original cast at the Planet Theater in Austin, Texas. In August of 1998 a performance was commissioned by ATHE (Association of Theater in Higher Education) at JumpStart Theater for its annual conference in San Antonio.

Characters

Emily	"High yellow" woman, indentured servant
Santa Anna	General Santa Anna, the middle-aged but still charismatic self-made emperor of Mexico
Sam Houston	Enigmatic leader of the Texianistas
Joe John Joshua	Slave, freed when master died at Alamo
Two Santanistas	Soldiers and soldaderas in Santa Anna's camp
Two Texianistas	Americans determined to take Texas by force. "Texianistas" is used for its comic effect as it relates to "Santanistas," but there is no historical precedent for its use.
Others	Old woman, Ladies, Concepción, Magdalena, David Crockett, James Bowie, Col. Morgan, Soldiers, etc.

Setting

Prologue and Epilogue: Philadelphia, 30 years after the Texas Revolution

Acts One and Two: Texas, between 1835 and 1836 during the Texas Revolution

Prologue

(Lights up on EMILY and TWO LADIES who sit stiffly in a parlor. They are all fiftyish and dressed for tea.)

1st LADY: My dear, these pastries are just scrumptious! I've never tasted anything quite like them before, have you Hortense?

2nd LADY: Truly, no. In all my years of taking tea, these take the cake. What do you call them?

EMILY: Empanadas. A Mexican delicacy.

1st LADY: Em-fa-NA-dias! How quaint. You are so fortunate to have Conception and Magdalena to cook, clean, and in general take care of you and your husband in your twilight years . . .

EMILY: We are indeed, blessed.

2nd LADY: . . . The servant problem here in Philadelphia is nothing short of a scandal.

1st LADY: But that shall surely change now that General Lee has surrendered. We should soon be getting a flood of good reliable colored help, anxious for honest work. (Clock strikes.) My, is that the right time? Where does it go? Come, my dear; we must be off. (THEY rise.)

2nd LADY: Thank you for tea, my dear. It was quite refined.

1st LADY: Don't you be a stranger Emily. You must come visit us soon. (LADIES exit.) *(EMILY rises and turns on music box. It plays a 'pop' version of the YELLO ROSE theme. EMILY does a stiff little dance. CONCEPCION and MAGDALENA rush in.)*

CONCEPCION: Mrs.! Mrs.! He's back again!

MAGDALENA: He won't go away! We told him to go, pero he won't go!

CONCEPCION: He says he's the best knife sharpener in the world, and he won't leave till he sharpens yours!

MAGDALENA: He's crazy; he says he knows you, Mrs.

EMILY: Knows me?

CONCEPCION: Si! Knows you from long ago. *(Stage whispers)* In TEXAS!

EMILY: You know you are forbidden to speak that word in my presence. Remember your promise, or I'll not hesitate to send you back where you came from.

MAGDALENA: Pues, that was almost thirty years ago. Everybody's forgotten about it already.

CONCEPCION: Everybody but you.

EMILY: You are wrong. I have forgotten, too. Do not remind me!

(JOE bursts in. The women gasp.)

JOE: That's my music. How did you get my music out of my heart and into a music box without me knowing about it?

CONCEPCION: You are confused Mr., eh . . . Mr. . . . .

JOE: Joe. Joe John . . .

EMILY: Joe John Joshua? I can't believe it?

MAGDALENA: You are confused Mr. Joe John Joshua.

CONCEPCION: This is a commercial music box, direct from New York City.

MAGDALENA: . . . And Mrs. has never been to Texas.

BOTH: Never! We promise.

EMILY: . . . although the song you hear does have Texas in the title... Perhaps my knives and scissors do need a bit of sharpening. Maggie, Connie, will you fetch them please? I will speak to this fellow.

BOTH : Yes, Mrs! *(They exit giggling.)*

JOE: *(Closes music box.)* I wrote that song! I wrote it for you when you were Emily Morgan before you became what you are now. It was my song all right, but sounds like somebody took it away.

EMILY: But how can music be stolen? I never realized . . .

JOE: Anything can get stolen around here, from the looks of it. Else, how could you stomach yourself passing for a white lady?

EMILY: Joe don't! You don't understand. You never did. I have had the life I wanted. Why shouldn't I have a respectable place in the world without being looked at like I was part monkey woman?

JOE: You are a respected woman now, is that it? But, what about respecting yourself?

EMILY: I don't need self-respect! I need to be able to breathe deeply without choking on the fumes of my own bitterness.

JOE: *(Whistles)* That there Ethiopian blood must be some powerful stuff. If the few drops it took to turn your white skin yellow are enough to transform your European heart.

(MAGDALENA and CONCEPCION enter arguing in Spanish, and carrying knives to be sharpened.)

CONCEPCION: No! 'Ta loca. No creo Santana tienen mas grandes huevos que Sam Houston! No way, José.

MAGDALENA: Pues, creo que si; pero, you think you know toda la 911.

CONCEPCION: Tell her, senora, that General Sam Houston was the bravest most macho general in La Revolution de Tejas . . .

MAGDALENA: No way! El hombre numero uno se fue General Antonio Lopez de Santa Anna, the Napoleon of the West, no less.

CONCEPCION: In your dreams, Mija. Tell her Mrs.You know the truth of it, verdad?

EMILY: I don't know what you mean. I must never speak of those times . . . I have forgotten myself.

JOE: Then, I will tell it!

MAGDALENA and CONCEPCION: YOU?!

JOE: I will tell it all. 'Cause I was there from the beginning, and I remember everything. Fact is, the whole thing started cause of me, if you want to know the truth. You see, that slave-owning, horse thief President Andrew Jackson, has his mind made up on Texas. He wanted it bad, for the riches and prestige it would bring him. Wanted it bad enough to kill for it, so he sent in a few of his hand picked special agents to initiate covert actions against the Mexican people.

CONCEPCION: I don't believe it!

JOE: Covert actions which led eventually to the overthrow of the sovereign government of Mexico . . .

MAGDALENA: Tell it like it is, mi hermano negro . . . !

EMILY: Must you talk of these things, Joe? Let them have their myth of heroes.

CONCEPCION: Yeah! It's all we got.

JOE: I care not to take your story away, but to tell my own. I am an old man who remembers everything. I especially remember you, Emily, meeting you in the chaos of revolution.

EMILY: But first a little background. Music professor!

(TEXIANISTAS sing)

> O Sam Houston where are you?
> Your nation needs you today!
> Mexico's taking back Texas—
> El Paso to Galveston Bay,
> Coahuila to Colorado,
> The story that has to be told
> Santana's taking back Texas—
> At the battle of El Alamo.

ACT ONE

Scene 1

(SAM sits isolated in light.)

SAM: Howdy. I'm Sam Houston. Freedom Fighter; agent of change. I'll be president some day just you wait. But you know; that slavery thing. It really bothers me. Deep in my heart it rattles and aches. The Mexican government had sense enough to outlaw it outright. But, there's still a brisk business 'round here in indentured servants with ninety-nine year leases. There's been many a black man I'd sooner have beside me in a close fight than quite a number of my own Anglo-Saxon race. Anybody who ever read the classics as I have, would recognize that the African possesses an old soul, with deep roots in the Cosmos. I understand. It's simple economics. They were built to withstand long hours working in the hellish sun, and somebody has to get the crops in. Folks in Europe are going naked for want of American Cotton. Economics, pure and simple. That, and an insatiable greed for adventure, greater even than the lust for land. In my formative years, you see, I lived among the Cherokee people, to live among them is to respect their ways. I am fortunately graced by an acquaintanceship with more than one way of life. *(Raises hand 'Indian style')* Howdy! I'm UtseTi Aretaski. That's my Indian name; means 'Big Drunk'. Not that I could do anything about it, of course. Slavery, I mean. After all I'm only one man, and my instincts tell me that now, is not the time to take a stand on that little issue. Still, it bothers the hell out of me. I swear to God. *(A pair of buckskin clad bumpkins wander in)* But meanwhile, duty calls . . . *(To men)* Howdy!

1st BUMPKIN: Howdy.

2nd BUMPKIN: How do . . .

SAM: Where're you boys from?

1st BUMPKIN: Kentucky and Alabama.

2nd BUMPKIN: Louisiana and Tennessee.

SAM: And you come to Texas soon as you heard about it, I bet.

1st BUMPKIN: Dang right! Heard there was cheap land, loose laws and purty señoritas.

2nd BUMPKIN: That's my recipe for happiness, might near.

SAM: How'd you boys like to come with me and kick Santana's ass? If we win, there's free land for the taking, and all the tail you can trim.

1st BUMPKIN: Santana? Sounds like a Mexican to me. Let's go get him.

2nd BUMPKIN: Sounds good, but ain't that a breech of international law? He's the president of Mexico, and Texas is still IN Mexico, strictly speaking.

SAM: Son, we owe it to Texas to take her away from the Mexicans. He'll never figure out what to do with her. We need her and she needs us. We got people coming. More and more every day . . . We outnumber the native born round here two to one already. My orders are coming from someone much higher than myself.

1st BUMPKIN: God Almighty?

SAM: No. Andy Jackson. President Jackson wants Texas, needs it like a drunk needs whisky, and by God, I'm gonna get it for him, if I have to kill every little brown person between here and the deep blue sea! Are you with me, boys? For Freedom and Free Land!?

1st BUMPKIN: Count me in!

2nd BUMPKIN: Me too. Let me at 'em!

SAM: Texas! Sweet Texas! Lying with her legs spread wide like La Chingada, wet and waiting for those big colonial cojones! Texas so like a woman; giving freely of her bounty sometimes, but other times, in need of a little coaxing . . . *(All three mount 'horses' and begin to mime riding which turns into humping.)* Texas! I'm coming for ya! The Spaniards grabbed her; the French kissed her; the Mexicans took her, and now, it's MY turn!! *(All three let out sigh of satisfaction as lights go to out.)*

Scene 2

(Streets of San Antonio. DAVID CROCKETT walks up to two Texas soldiers)

DAVY: Can one of you boys tell me where I might find General Samuel Houston?

2nd SOLDIER: Ole' Sam's out east with his army trying to hold on to Texas . . .

DAVY: Tell him Col. Crockett has arrived and his troubles are just about over.

1st SOLDIER: You ain't no Davy Crockett!

2nd SOLDIER: If you're Davy Crockett, I'm John Wayne and this here's my side-kick Andy Divine!

1st SOLDIER: Everybody knows that ole' Davy always sports a coonskin tail hat and a fringy buckskin suit!

DAVY: No, no, that was Daniel Boone, you ignorant fellow. History will forever confuse me with that lucky bumpkin. I am not 'Davy', but DAVID Crockett. I have never sported a coon-skin, and in fact, all fir makes me sneeze up a storm. As for buckskin, I love what Ralph Lauren has done with it this year, but I prefer for myself, a nice cut-away gabardine.

2nd SOLDIER: Well, I don't know . . .

DAVY: I promise you that I am Col. David Crockett, former U.S. Congressman, raconteur, fearless Indian killer, and a runaway slave's worse nightmare. I've come, like you I suppose, to kill a few little Mexicans in the name of American economic policy.

1st SOLDIER: If you're really Davy Crockett, how old was you when you kilt your first bear?

DAVY: Only three.

2nd SOLDIER: What was your major accomplishment in Congress?

DAVY: I patched up the crack in the Liberty Bell.

1st SOLDIER: By, God it IS you!

2nd SOLDIER: Hot Damn, Davy! I'm your Tennessee homeboy too!

DAVY: Listen boys, I hope you've learned something from this. I am not 'DAVY'. I am not my image. I am David. An image is a thing, like a movie star's persona. Mixing me up with the other is quite dangerous. It reminds me of the story of . . .

1st SOLDIER: Sam Houston's army's all full up. You'll have to settle for Travis, Bowie, and the Alamo fort. We could sure use another martyr for white supremacy.

2nd SOLDIER: 'Specially such a famous one. Everybody's heard of YOU. Seen your plays . . .

1st SOLDIER: Read your books . . .

2nd SOLDIER: Col. Travis will be SO impressed.

1st SOLDIER: Talk about your effete snobs . . . But he is a plucky little devil, I'll give him that.

2nd: Col. Bowie's too sick to command. They say it's consumption.

1st SOLDIER: . . . But knowing his ways, it's more likely syphilis.

2nd: He's in a sick-room with his curandera.

1st SOLDIER: She might as well give him last rights, I expect.

DAVY: Take me to him, before it's too late!

2nd: Sure thing, Davy; but would you do us a favor and put this on. *(Hands DAVY coon-skin cap)* . . . Just so there'll be no embarrassing questions . . .

1st SOLDIER: Yeah.

(DAVY takes hat, starts to put it on, then throws it down and jumps up and down on it.)

Scene 3

(LOVE THE LAND theme, instrumental. After the battle, two SANTANISTA soldiers stack 'bodies' of Alamo heroes into pile for burning.)

1st SANTANISTA: Pinché cabrones! How come we get all the shit detail? First it was grinding the masa for El Presidente's tortillas, and now . . .

2nd: Now we have to clean these stupid dead heroes of the Alamo. If it wasn't so hot around here, I might desert.

1st: De veras, hombre. Where you from, 'vato'?

2nd: Quere'taro; se fue un campasino, Chinga el sorteo!

1st: Soy de San Luis. They drafted my ass, tambien. It was my quempleanos, y todos la familia, y los gentes locales bebemos en la cantana. We got muy pedo. Next thing I knew, I was in the army, dude.

2nd: Orale' tambien, and marching a thousand miles to kill los norteamericano invaders. Why don't they just go back where they came from, if they don't like it here in Mexico?

1st: Verdad! We didn't tell them to come to this chinga place. Why do they want too, anyway? It's too pinche hot.

2nd: You said it!

1st: They'll never amount to anything until they get some climate control. Tengo muy sed.

2nd: . . . And these pinche heros smell bad; even for Gringos. *(An Old Woman enters.)*

OLD WOMAN: What are you all doing? Stacking up those heroes like cordwood! You ought to be ashamed! These boys deserve a Christian burial.

1st: Look lady, we'got orders to burn 'em.

2nd: That's the fate of dead traitors. At least it keeps the buzzards away, que no?

OLD WOMAN: Savages! You'll burn in hell for this blasphemy.

2nd: De veras, vieja, but hell ain't no worse than South Texas! *(She exits.)*

1st: A raspa would really hit the spot right now.

2nd: Sorry, hombré; you're about a hundred and fifty years too early!

(Lights dim, x-fade to SANTA ANNA's tent.)

(TEXIANISTAS sing)

> O Sam Houston where are you?
> Your nation needs you today!
> Mexico's taking back Texas--
> El Paso to Galveston Bay,
> Coahuila to Colorado,
> The story that has to be told
> Santana's taking back Texas--
> At the battle of El Alamo.
> (Lights cross fade to Santa Anna)

Scene 4

(SANTA ANNA has supper in his tent after the Battle of El Alamo.)

SANTA ANNA: Nothing like the scent of fresh blood to sharpen the appetite. Nopalitos and Calabasa con javalina a la parrilla. All growing wild in this region. Is this not the garden of Eden? I love mi tierra bonita. And to think, amigo, these pinche Texianistas have the unmitigated arrogance to think they can steal our ancestral lands out from under us simply because God told them it was okay? What do they take us for? Indians? I will crush them. I have an army of ten thousand warriors thirsty for their gringo blood. I will strike at the heart of these audacious intruders with the savage might of my nation's fury. This Alamo business. This is nothing but small tamales, business as usual. Swatting mosquitoes that mistake themselves for eagles. These bastards stung quite a number of my good soldiers too, including my barber. No quarter! Asked or given. Five or six survivors were brought before me, after I had told those pendejos over and over 'no prisoners!' One of them was that woodsman, the Great Indian Fighter, como se yama, David' Crockéte. He demanded the mercy of an honorable death, claimed he was a congressman, as if that was a license to lawbreak! I ordered him shot on the spot. Beheaded and thrown on the pile with the other traitors. No quarter does not mean 'con su permisso.' Tomorrow we will head east and seek that upstart

Sam Houston and his rebel outlaws. Migelito! More wine! Do you want me to die of thirst in this hell hole?!

(SANTA ANNA and SANTANISTAS sing)

> I love the land!
> For los mountains and valleys
> I'll fight to the death to defend
> Till I'm the last standing man.
> Me and the land.
> And together we'll build us a nation
> Where freedom takes power
> And Justice alone takes command.
> Please Understand.
> In the world of my dreaming made real
> By the seemingly endless reserves of my will,
> Free to kill to be free, free to kill to be free
> To be sure it's all right, free to fight, free to kill,
> It's all right!
> If I have to I'll happily hurt you
> So try to stay, out of my sight.
> Please Understand.
> In the world of my dreaming made real
> By the seemingly, endless reserves of my will,
> Free to kill to be free, free to kill to be free
> To be sure it's all right, free to fight, free to kill,
> It's all right!
> If I have to I'll happily hurt you
> So try to stay out of my sight.

Scene 5

(The home of COL. JAMES MORGAN, wealthy patriot, ex–Northerner, and developer of Texas lands, at the mouth of the San Jacinto River. He sits at parlor table with SAM.)

MORGAN: Are you quite sure Sam? Could there be some mistake in communication'?

SAM: None, Col. Morgan. We have spies. He's headed this way, all right. Heading for me and my army. Should be to Morgan's Point by sundown day after tomorrow. You just have the bad luck to be between us and him, and I guarantee you he'll want to stop by to pick up a souvenir or two.

MORGAN: I will advise the servants to begin packing. Surely, he will not harm our womenfolk, for I hear he has the disposition of a gentleman.

SAM: Do not be swayed by his love of lace and silver chamber pots, for he is as cold a killer as the greatest Roman general cold and driven by relentless demons. His history is muddied by many contradictions.

MORGAN: Don't tell me you believe that story about the squaw and the patriarch of the greatest family in Kentucky? That this same Santana is the bastard offspring of that cursed union?

SAM: This is Texas, Col. Morgan. We've come to expect the unusual. And sure you know, sir, that one of my wives is a full Cherokee.

MORGAN: Sam, I meant you no disrespect.

SAM: The best years of my life were spent among her people. They have a sure fine notion of the important things in this world.

MORGAN: Pray, why did you leave this paradise?

SAM: Figured I better get out among my own and do what I could to keep the white man's guns
from wiping out their nation . . . Do you read much, Col.? History? Philosophy?

MORGAN: Not much time for that sort of thing with a wife and two daughters growing more
troublesome with each day; and after all, we are a working farm and ranch with over 100 animals, 17 slaves, eh servants; indentured servants in the fields and 10 in the household, so not only am I husband, father, and lord of the manor, I am the chief of a small village with the health and welfare of every living creature on my head.

SAM: When you read the history of the world, Col. Morgan, the nature of things as they are between the lines. It really makes you stop and think. Whether Santana is a Spanish noble, a peon, or the very son of Satan, he has certainly put the fear of God in these Texian

Freedom Fighters. He's cut off our supplies, out maneuvered our re-enforcements, and killed some of our finest young boys, without showing mercy for their tender years or their mother's breaking hearts. And on top of that, he has the shamelessness to go about looking like a durn Paris dandy astride a white horse.

(*EMILY enters with serving tray. She and SAM stare at each other for a moment before she remembers her duty and places glasses on tray.*)

MORGAN: Thank you, Emily. Oh Sam, have you not had the pleasure of meeting . . .

SAM: . . . your young daughter! I see the favor in her . . .

MORGAN: (*Interrupting*) My servant, Emily, an indentured bondswoman, from far away New York.

SAM: . . . Beg your pardon.

EMILY: General Houston. I am honored to meet so legendary a warrior for justice.

MORGAN: Your reputation as an opponent of slavery has preceded you, Sam.

SAM: Miss Emily, such a heartfelt compliment from so charming a lady is a double joy. I am pleased you share my convictions that Texas remains a free territory.

EMILY: I am a free-born mulatto woman, sir, never chained nor whipped. But in a land of slaves, I am merely one more for the shackles.

SAM: What a crime against mankind to have you locked in bondage.

EMILY: And so it is, indeed for the least of us. Is that all Col. Morgan?

MORGAN: Yes, thank you my dear. (*She goes.*) As you see, she has quite a mind of her own. We treat her like one of the family. My girls adore her.

SAM: I can sure see why. The hour grows late. I must get back to my men; we expect news from Travis at any time. (*Aside*) For those of you who are trying to follow the story. You and yours, Colonel, need to pack-up and git.

MORGAN: Godspeed you Sam! We'll send our food and useful goods to your camp.

SAM: Thank you, sir; and watch out for that rascal Santana. He's a sly fox. *(Lights down)*

Scene 6

(Cross fade to SANTA ANNA on the road to San Jacinto. He is riding his white horse, eating opium, and talking aloud to himself.)

SANTA ANNA: These rustics dare to make a monster out of me! These low bumpkins have the balls to cast me as the barbarian of the piece, when it is they that have so grossly abused our gracious hospitality by trying to steal the land on which they have been allowed to live as naturalized citizens. We treated them like guests. Don't talk to me about boorish behavior! I'm tired of these arrogant shits. No quarter! Kill all of them con gusto and then piss on their corpses. Throw them in a pile and burn them like the carcasses of diseased cattle! I am the leader of a Great Nation that swarms with angry people. They are angry with themselves; they are angry with me. But most of all, they are angry with this gang of land-grabbing Anglo-Saxon invaders carrying on like backwoods conquistadors! No quarter! None! I want all of them dead before me. Except for the women and children, of course. And the blacks. Those who wish to be patriots may join my army. Let the others run free to warn their former masters that Santana is coming with his beautiful army, and he has not had a woman in three days!

Scene 7

(EMILY and JOE are packing supplies and preparing to vacate Morgan's Point.)

EMILY: That should be the last of it. Hurry Joe; help me with these candlesticks. Poor Mrs. Morgan was in such a mad rush. I know she didn't mean to leave them.

JOE: I'm hurrying Miss Emily. I don't want to meet up with that devil again this side of hell.

EMILY: Not' Miss'. I'm just Emily. You're a freedman now Joe. Besides, I'm just as black as you, for all my golden skin.

JOE: Sorry, Mi . . . Emily. I forgot you ain't no white lady.

EMILY: Please, Joe; I shall never bare that burden. How did James Bowie treat you? Did he
make you sharpen his knife?

JOE: That's in the past. Dead like him. Right now, I cain't think of nothing but the future, and how to make sure you're part of mine.

EMILY: How, downright courtly of you. But this is not the time for us, is it? Don't you sense that? *(They embrace and kiss.)*

JOE: *(Shouts and shooting off)* MY GOD in the morning!

EMILY: Let's run for our lives! They're killing everybody! (*SANTANISTA soldiers burst in with drawn swords.*) Have mercy!

1st SOLD.: Do not worry my paloma. El President does not kill contraband persons. And you will be a welcome captive. I might even get promoted to sarge. Move out! *(Exit at sword point. 2nd SOLDIER gathers up candlesticks and other loot. Lights out.)*

(Song: "Yellow Rose" theme, instrumental)

Scene 8

(JOE is alone in a P.O.W. tent, a guard returns with EMILY.)

JOE: You O.K.? He didn't mess with you, did he?

EMILY: I'm fine. He wants to have dinner with me.

JOE: He wants to have YOU for dinner.

EMILY: But can he stomach such a salty dish?

JOE: Why you talk like that? You know it drives me crazy! *(He clumsily nuzzles her.)*

EMILY: No time for that stuff now; we got plenty to do before tomorrow. I bribed a soldier to leave a horse for you tied on the eastern edge of the bivouac. Ride him as fast as you can to Sam Houston's camp. He's in the river bend, about eight miles past Morgan's Point. Think you can find it?

JOE: Sure I can.

EMILY: Good. Give him this map. It tells him exactly where we are, and how many there are here. Tell him all is well and in God's hands. I will preoccupy the General as best I can till he can get here.

JOE: You want me to leave you here alone with Santana! I can't do that.

EMILY: You can and you must, Joe. Nothing less than the future of Texas rides with you.

JOE: I'll be back before tomorrow night has come.

EMILY: I hope you will, and have Sam Houston with you. I told Santana that Houston was about three hundred miles north. He won't be ready for battle for days.

JOE: I'll ride like the wind. So long.

JOE: (*Riding to Sam's camp that night. Music under.*) I'm Joe. I'm John. Sometimes I'm Joshua, too. They all inside me. Probably more. I escaped death and became a free man fighting for slave Texas. Jim Bowie bought me from the famous Jean Laffite. Gave me this big ole' frog-sticker when he croaked. Travis made me come along so he could feel more the gentlemen with a slave beside him fighting for his right to hold slaves. That was John talking. Hollywood showed him taking it in the back to shield his good master Jim Bowie from a Mexican bayonet. But he's here. Inside me. I'm Joshua now, I feel his young sap flowing like first love. You remember me? For how long. And I'm still Joe too, don't forget. If I could do what I WANT to do, I'd quick as lightening join the Santanistas, and when this war is over, high-tail it down the gulf coast of Mexico till I got to Vera Cruz. Vera Cruz! Just across the gulf from my Island cousins. We could start a fellowship of new world free black people. I would learn their rhythms, and I would teach them a more judicious use of spice. Together we would unite in triumph over the diaspora!! But just like Hollywood, I'll stay here and be the revolution's errand boy. Just so I can be near the one

I love. I do love Emily, you know. Love her so much I'll go against my own better judgment to help her out. But ain't that what love's all about?

(Sings)

> There's a yellow rose in Texas
> My true love she will be
> No other dark man knows her
> No white man; only me
> She's the sweetest rose of color
> That the world shall ever know
> Until the day I join her
> My poor heart is full of woe.
> You can talk about your Lily Mae
> And sing of Rosa Lee.
> But the High Yellow Rose of Texas
> She's the one, dear one for me!
> I love a coal-black woman
> And a fancy fine fair brown;
> But a fair, fine-hair high-yellow
> Sure to get my damper down;
> She's the queen of chocolate bayou,
> She's honey from the bee;
> She's the High Yellow Rose of Texas,
> And together we'll be free.

Scene 9

(Houston's camp. SAM has just finished reading mail. JOE stands near.)

SAM: You are a brave man, young Joe. With this intelligence, we might be able to catch ole' Santana with his britches down. How is Miss Emily?

JOE: Emily is well enough. I can't wait to get her out of Texas--her and me both. No offense, sir.

SAM: None taken. Emily is my idea of a patriot. Self-sacrifice is her true nature. I don't blame you for wanting to go, however. Texas is inhabited by a heap of hard-headed hombres bound and determined to see you both in legal bondage. I'm again'it, but I'm only one man, and I learned long ago not to make long term promises. Ask the Cherokee about promises. Utseti Arataski knows about promises.

SOLDIERS: You tell 'em, Big Drunk.

SAM: I just want you to know that, in my book, both you and Emily are heroes of the revolution. That's a fact. It's a damn shame nobody will ever know about it.

JOE: I hear you, sir.

SAM: Grab yourself some grub, young Joe. We ride at dawn tomorrow. (*JOE exits*) What is there about this place, these people, that draws me heart and soul into their conflict? Andy Jackson, it's all your damn fault. There I was living a perfect full life, and Andy sent me down here to cogitate with the local Cherokees, a splendid people by the way, to make sure they didn't take sides with Santana, in this war, and by durn if I don't end up general of a revolutionary army. Must be pure fate. Those old Greeks believed in it sure enough, Homer, Odysseus. It's a handy explanation for the unexplainable. If fate would have it that my army of farmers and traveling rogues is to do battle with the mighty Santa Anna and his legions, then so be it. There's a lot of real estate hanging in the balance. What we lack in uniforms and fit victuals, we more than make up in our dogged determination to live free to establish free enterprise or die trying. When it comes right down to it . . .

(SAM and TEXIANS sing)

> I love the land.
> For its cotton, tobacco and sugar cane
> Good grazing grain
> Makes me feel good again.
> Try to understand.
> That a man needs his African labor
> To plant in the summer
> Tend to the children and
> Harvest his land.
> So I'll fight for the right to be free
> Free to kill to be free

Free to fight when I'm right
In God's sight!
Free to kill, it's all right.
In the wisdom of God we all trust
'Cause he's a White Man like us!

(*Lights out*)

END OF ACT ONE

ACT TWO

Scene 1

(The following afternoon. SANTA ANNA and EMILY in his tent. Candlelight and fine fixtures in a luxurious setting. SANTA ANNA is dressed in white silks under a velvet dressing gown decorated with medals. EMILY is in a fancy 'captured' dress and jewelry.)

SANTA ANNA: Turn around slowly and let me examine you in detail. Ah yes! You glow like a yellow rose in the moonlight. God has heard my prayers.

EMILY: More champagne, señor? More tamales? *(She serves him.)*

SANTA ANNA: Do you think me a clown? A fool?

EMILY: No, Excellency! One does not become Emperor of Mexico by accident. You have surely earned the title.

SANTA ANNA: As sanguine as you are beauteous, my blossom.

EMILY: Do you flatter all your prisoners so?

SANTA ANNA: Only those who dare to take my heart prisoner. Stop serving me. Come. Come sit beside me. I want to kiss your lips. I want to taste you. *(She sits and they kiss.)*

EMILY: Well?

SANTA ANNA: Like honeysuckle and rose over an open flame. *(They kiss more passionately.)* Here in this tent, there is no world but the world we make. You are no longer a slave, a servant. You are a woman here by her own will. Why do you smile such a smile?

EMILY: Forgive me, but it is so odd to find myself here making love to the enemy General among the finery of my former life.

SANTA ANNA: You have shed no tears for your slain masters? Are you thus coldhearted?

EMILY: My tears are for the living.

SANTA ANNA: You are a woman like no other. I confess; I have not known the tender companionship of your sex for more than three days. For a voluptuary like myself, this is an eternity! And you are a rich capriotada for the breaking of so long a fast . . .

EMILY: You are no celibate. I have seen the soldaderas in your camp. I've listened to them giving relief to your battle happy, soldiers.

SANTA ANNA: Oh they are very well for my army, but I never touch them. They are crawling with lice. I have awaited your capture.

EMILY: They are no doubt true; the things that they say about you. . . .

SANTA ANNA: What things'? I am always interested in what pretty women say about me.

EMILY: All manner of things, Excellency . . .

SANTA ANNA: Tell me, dammit. Such talk causes my sap to rise.

EMILY: Well, Excellency . . .

SANTA ANNA: Toñio. Please call me Toñio, querida.

EMILY: Well, Toñio, they say you are richer than George Washington and possess the spirit of the fighting bull between your strong legs . . .

SANTA ANNA: The BULL? I prefer to compare my passion to the graceful brutality of the mountain lion. The Sacred Jaguar of Aztlan!

EMILY: Some say that you are not even Mexicano, but a half-breed adventurer from Kentuck.

SANTA ANNA: Bah! I have heard these stories. That I went to West Point, that I was half Indian! How could both be true? I hate Indians. The only thing I hate worse than Indians is white people!

EMILY: We can no more properly call them 'Indians' Toñio, indeed this land is not India.

SANTA ANNA: De veras, Rosa mio. They should be called Americans, for is this not their homeplace? These Anglos won't even admit to Columbo's errors in judgment. How can they be expected to address their own? Do you like silk, my dove of the arroyos?

EMILY: Yes, of course. It's like heaven.

SANTA ANNA: So do I, my dear, so do I. I like it better than anything except the sight of my enemy's blood. Come, feel my silk shirt.
Yes. Touch my silk underpants, they hold a stiff arrow aimed at your
sweet target . . . *(Lights out)*

Scene 2

*(That next afternoon. Two SANTANISTA guards stand before the closed
tent. Noises come from inside.)*

SANTA ANNA *(From within)* Rosa! Mi Rosa!!

EMILY: X-X- Excellency! Excellenceeeee!

1st SANTANISTA: How long can they go on like that?

2nd SANTANISTA: It's disgusting, no? I can't even hear myself
think.

(Noises, shouts within)

1st SANTANISTA: It's too hot to be doin' the nasty.

2nd SANTANISTA: Somebody better tell the Generalissimo. Has
he got los grandes cojones, or what, vato?

(More noise within)

1st SANTANISTA: It they don't stop pretty soon, I'm going to
have to find me a ruca. Why should we be the only two pendejos not
enjoying ourselves.

2nd SANTANISTA: You're right, Carnal; everybody's either sleeping or getting busy.

1st SANTANISTA: It's too hot to fight anyway.

2nd SANTANISTA: Hell, let's go join the fiesta! He'll never miss
us!

1st: Vamonos! Ha! Ha! *(They exit.)*

SANTA ANNA: My, dam is breaking again; it's about to flood your
valley!

EMILY: Hold on one more momento, my bull of the mountains; my storm clouds are almost ready to release their rain . . . !

(SHOUTS off. "Remember the Alamo!!" "Remember Goliad "Remember Pearl Harbor!" "ME no Alamo!" "Me no Pearl Harbor!!!")

SANTA ANNA: *(Coming out of tent)* What th . . . Holy shit! *(SHOUTS: The enemy is come! Run for your lives!)* You! You have done this Emily! *(He tries to dress.)* How could you? You have deliberately delayed your climax in order to give Sam Houston more time to advance!

EMILY: *(Comes out of tent)* It's better this way, Toñio . . .

SANTA ANNA: I am General Antonio Lopez de Santa Anna! Emperor of All Mexico! Napoleon of the West! It is not my destiny to die here today in the company of a spying whore. If I had more time, I'd kill you. Adios, puta! As long as the prickly pear blooms this land will forever be MEXICO . . .! Because . . . *(Sings)* I Love the Land . . . !

(Shouts of 'Remember the Alamo' as he runs off)

EMILY: So like a man, to leave a lady lacking. *(TEXIANS and SAM enter)* SAM!

SAM: Emily Morgan. We meet again.

EMILY: Did you catch the General? He ran off that way.

SAM: We'll take him in due time. I, and all the freedom loving people of Texas, owe you a debt, Emily. We took them in a rout, thanks to the distraction you provided.

EMILY: I did it in the hope that the Morgan family will once again inhabit Morgan's Point. And in gratitude, I may be granted free passport back north.

SAM: If there be any favor, large or small that I may do, count it done.

EMILY: Perhaps. Perhaps one. We shall see how small it turns out to be . . .

(She leads him back into tent.)

(SANTANISTAS sing)

O Santana where are you?
Your country needs you God knows
Sam Houston's taking our Texas
And taking sweet Emily Rose. . . .

Scene 3

(After the battle, two Textianista soldiers pick through the bodies of dead and dying Santanistas.)

1st TEXIANISTA: We sure kilt a bunch of them buggers, by damn! How many you think there is?

2nd TEXIANISTA: Too damn many to bury, I know that for a fact.

1st TEXIANISTA: You're right about that. This here ground's gonna stink like grease for a hundred years.

2nd TEXIANISTA: You think Mexicans have souls like regular folks?

1st TEXIANISTA: I reckon the good ones must go to some Mexican style heaven, full up with candles and purty statues.

2nd TEXIANISTA: Lookey there! A gold snuff box!

1st TEXIANISTA: By damn if it ain't! Better get all you can off'em now, Brother, cause by tomorrow they'll be starting to smell like rotten tamale shit.

2nd TEXIANISTA: You're right about that, brother! *(Pulls out a pair of pliers.)*

1st TEXIANISTA: What's them for, Brother?

2nd TEXIANISTA: I can get two-bits a piece for Mexican teeth! *(He yanks out teeth from corpse.)*

1st TEXIANISTA: Brother, you are one crazy peckerwood! *(Senorita walks by with babe in arms and searches through bodies.)*

1st TEXIANISTA: Lookit! Ain't that one right pretty señorita!

2nd TEXIANISTA: By golly, I could sure suck on that little chile bean. (*They begin circling her and touching her body.*)

1st TEXIANISTA: Ain't it queer how Mexican senoritas is fine and docile like as a spring born pup . . .

2nd TEXIANISTA: And their men is such mongrel scum . . . (*They grab her.*)

WOMAN: No! Por favor, no puedo! Yo no soy soldadera, soy la esposa de un coronel muerto! Ay Dios! (*Both men rape her on top of corpses.*)

1st TEXIANISTA: Remember the Alamo!

2nd TEXIANISTA: Relax and enjoy it!

WOMAN: No! (*She curses them in Spanish.*)

Scene 4

(*JOE in his cabin preparing to flee. Sings*)

> She's the sweetest rose of color,
> You ever want to see.
> She's the High Yellow Rose of Texas,
> Gonna run away with me!

(*Speaks*) Yes, by gumption, I'm outta here at sundown, gonna meet up with Emily and me and my gal gonna head way way down south till we get to the Islands! Then we gonna open up ourselves a knife sharpening business. Together we gone hone happiness out of dull, rusty discontent. We gonna . . . (*A loud knock*) Who knocks yonder? (*SANTA ANNA enters*)

SANTA ANNA: Forgive me, but I find myself in a rather embarrassing situation. You see. I must have your clothes.

JOE: My clothes? These clothes I'm wearing?

SANTA ANNA: You may take mine. Except, of course, for my diamond-studded shirt.

JOE: I don't know . . .

SANTA ANNA: *(Pulls out pistol and points it at JOE.)* I'm afraid I must insist. I would hate to make a hole in the chest of a compadre . . .

JOE: *(Steps behind screen)* O.K., but I'm keeping my brogans . . . !

SANTA ANNA: I knew I could count on your good judgment. *(They begin to exchange clothes.)* You may not think so at this moment, my friend, but today is your lucky day. Now you can tell your grandchildren that you have swapped duds with The Napoleon of the West. Did you know it was I?

JOE: Sure. I saw you real clear after that Alamo mission fight. Guess I owe you a debt of thanks for killing everybody there and making me a free man as a result. But it don't seem right somehow.

SANTA ANNA: Ah yes! The Alamo. An inadequate, suicidal fortification, but an excellent tourist attraction in the making . . .

JOE: What'll you do now? High tail it down to Mexico City?

SANTA ANNA: I have a feeling I might not be 'man of the hour' in la cuidad, if you know what I mean. As a result of Texas being stolen by Houston and his pirates. I have lost one third of my nation's territory, turning thousands of my people into instant foreigners in the land of their birth! I'd do well to let things cool down a bit before returning to El Capital . . .

JOE: I hear the Islands are real nice this time of year. Balmy and calm; people of every color, good food! Rum! I'm going there with my woman! Just as soon as I tell her, wait and see!

SANTA ANNA: Women! *(Spits)* I'm through with them! For a while, it was a woman who has placed me in my present predicament--a yellow, spying beauty that used her charms on me to assist that traitorous felon Sam Houston in stealing my country from its rightful owners. With my superior numbers and skills at battle, he never would have taken me. Never! If only I had not been in afternoon delicto with La Rosa Amarilla!

JOE: Sounds to me like not the woman's blame, but your own lusty nature's.

SANTA ANNA: I must keep my senses sharpened to a fine point in order to operate at peak level. But what do you know about a man of destiny like myself. You, a humble sharpener of other people's knives . . .

JOE: My own, too, sometimes; notwithstanding.

SANTA ANNA: *(The exchange is complete. BOTH step from behind screens.)* The Islands, you say? Perhaps not so bad a haven for a while . . . Quien sabés? There now. Do I not make a convincing beggar?

JOE: Except for your diamond studs . . .

SANTA ANNA: Oh, yes. How's that now? Perhaps I should stoop my shoulders a bit more. And frown.

JOE: That's it. That's pitiful.

SANTA ANNA: No sacrifice of dignity is too great, in the name of patriotism. Bueños suretes, mon ami. *(Exits)*

Scene 5

(SAM is sitting under an oak tree. His legs are extended and one of his feet is bandaged. TEXIANISTAS bring in SANTA ANNA at gunpoint.)

SAM: Well General Santa Anna, as I live and breathe!

SANTA ANNA: General Sam Houston, as I hope to do, too. *(There is a stiff pause.)*

SAM: Well, sientete, for land's sakes. I can't get up to shake your hand, though I'd damn well like to.

SANTA ANNA: You have been wounded.

SAM: It's a little nothing! Escopeta ball hit my Achilles tendon. It just means I'll never walk straight again, is all.

SANTA ANNA: It least it was not your balls, eh?

SAM: By damn, general, you are a pistol! Ha! Ha! Ha! Ouch!

SANTA ANNA: You are in pain. How sad.

SAM: You really don't know how sad. I've sworn off the hootch for the duration of this little war, and I ate the last of my opium yesterday morning. *(HE sobs.)*

SANTA ANNA: Ah, my general, the Gods of the East have smiled upon you! *(He produces stash from his pant leg.)* I managed to spirit away a plug or two for my intended escape.

SAM: Glory be to Goddamm! I'll feel like my old self again, thanks to the valiant enemy chief. *(He chews drug.)* Ummmm! I do like eating it, don't you? Smoking it is such a waste, with all due respect to my Chinese brothers, half of it goes up in smoke to stone the birds. Thanks general.

SANTA ANNA: It is the least I can do for the Great General Houston, for you have captured The Napoleon of the West!

1st TEXIANISTA: If he hadn't been crying so loud, we would'a never found him under that bridge, Sam.

2nd TEXIANISTA: I didn't know who he was . . .

1st TEXIANISTA: Hell, I didn't either! But I knew he must be some damn body with them diamond fuckin' buttons all down his shirt front.

2nd TEXIANISTA: . . . Then we marched him here by the prisoners and they started hollering "Mira, mira! El Presidente!

BOTH: El Presidente!!

SAM: That musta cooked your sauce, huh general?

SANTA ANNA: What will you do with me? Remember I am the commander-in-chief of a sovereign nation with European allies.

SAM: Some of the boys want to 1ynch you from a cottonwood tree and use you for target practice . . .

SANTA ANNA: What a joker . . . !

SAM: But I think I'll take you up to Washington, and hook you up with Ole' Hickory.

SANTA ANNA: Tie me to a tree? Is this some strange Norte Americano ritual?

SAM: Andy Jackson. Andy Jackson the President of the United States of America. By loosing so handily, you've added a great deal to the land he can now legally call his own.

SANTA ANNA: Oh yes! The President on the Jax Beer label! I admire his taste.

SAM: Bet he would surely love to display you in congress. Let the press play it up big. He's running for re-election, you know. Conquered dictators are real vote-getters.

SANTA ANNA: I will have to have new uniforms, of course. *(1st TEX. brings him clean uniform coat.)* And medals. You did manage to confiscate my medals, I hope.

(SAM motions and 2nd TEX. produces a small chest. He gives it to SANTA ANNA.)

SANTA ANNA: Ah*! (HE opens chest and holds up medal.)* They are like my children! This one was from the immortal campaign of 1813. How glorious it was! Blood and purple fire. I will gladly meet with your illustrious president, as his humble captive, if you will answer me one question, it has been bothering me for days now. That Alamo business? What in the world were they thinking? They seemed determined to be slaughtered. I was forced to oblige.

SAM: And they'll be holding that one against you for many years, Generalissimo . . .

SANTA ANNA.:   But they were begging for it! Like a child willing to test your patience with annoying behavior just to see how long it will take you to slap him.

SAM: I have children too; I hear you.

SANTA ANNA: I must confess, I needed a victory badly, so it couldn't have come at a better
time. You do understand, no?

SAM: I do. I needed the loss, too. A massacre is a great motivator of men, you know. Besides, war is not for lily livers.

SANTA ANNA: Sir! I am no coward! I am strong and brave enough to withstand the bitter assault of that cruel word in order that I may survive to fulfill my destiny. For he who runs away assures himself of at least the possibility of a long life.

SAM: Hell, I hope you live to be a wrinkled old white-head. I'm a big fan of your country, you know. A nation of riches whose greatest treasure is a strong determined people. I might rule it myself someday, don't be surprised.

SANTA ANNA: I must admire your arrogance, señor, and your tolerance for opium.

SAM: Pain's all but gone. Help me up boys. *(He stands, assisted by TEXIANISTAS.)* Yes sir, can't you just see me! Emperor of the Greatest nation in the civilized world stretching from Canada to the Yucatan. If Andy Jackson backs me up, I could take Mexico City with five thousand ruthless men. Don't worry. I'll appoint you Ambassador to the Court of St. James.

SANTA ANNA: But London is so dreary.

SAM: After all, let's face it: you and I have more in common than not. I figured it out a long time ago, Santana ole'pal. Some men were just born to take a leadership position.

(Lights change. An OLD WOMAN interrupts. She is Anglo and poor.)

OLD WOMAN: Sam Houston! Sam Houston!! You clean up these Mexican corpses at once, you hear me?! This might be a battlefield to you but it happens to be my farm, and I'll not have it polluted up with these durn dead stinking Mexicans!

SAM: Madame, I sympathize with your plight. But I have no men for gravedigging. Besides which, my boys hate them worse than they hate Indians.

OLD WOMAN: I've got planting to do! You expect me to plow them under like dry cornstalks?!

SAM: Why not? He'll make excellent compost for your crop. It's all a part of the great circle of life and death. In and out; in and out...

OLD WOMAN: Ahaaaaaahwa!

(SANTA ANNA speaks to SAM.)

SANTA ANNA: Allow me to handle her, compadre, for I have had much experience subduing unruly citizens. Madame, have a care how you address your betters, for you are here only by our grace! You exist at our pleasure. So grand is our personal vision, that it has the power to spin history's great wheel, or if we so desire, to bring it to a grinding halt. Do you like silk? Come with me my little cucaracha . . . *(They exit together.)*

JOE: *(Enters running)* General Sam! General Sam! She's gone! She left without so much as a so long I'll see you later. My Emily! Why did she do it? Why?

SAM: There, there, Joe boy. That woman has plans that don't include any of us, I hazard.

JOE: But I love her! I can't help myself from doing it. *(Sobs)*

SAM: Come on, pull yourself back together in one piece . . .

JOE: It ain't right! I ought to get the woman! That's the way it should be this time. For me! After all my trials, am I again to end up with nothing?

SAM: You've still got your black skin . . .

JOE: Nothing but my black skin? My GOD! This world ain't nothing but an ongoing torture from the first time you breathe the air; cause the air you breathe is the only thing in your life not trying to kick you down . . . !

SAM: Don't speak so eloquently about your suffering, boy; you'll only perpetuate it.

JOE: I even made up a song about her. Made it up from my heart. Never got to sing it for her . . . Now I'll never sing it!

SAM: Sing it for me. Lord knows I could use a tune.

JOE *(Sings)*

> I love a coal black woman
> And a fancy, fine fair-brown
> But a fair, fine-hair high-yellow
> Sure to get my damper down.
> She's the queen of Chocolate Bayou

She's honey from the bee
She's the High Yellow Rose of Texas and
Together we'll be free . . .

(During song, actors 'age' and change into prologue costumes)

SAM: I reckon that's about the end of my usefulness to this little operetta. From the looks of things, I'd say we were about ready to go back to real time, 1866. I was three years dead by then, so I'll just be moseying back to that great bye and bye. By the time this music ends, I gotta be gone so, see you over there... Oh! As for that little 'co ones' question raised early on. Think about it. The right answer will come easy . . . *(SAM disappears. Music concludes.)*

Epilogue

JOE: That's all of it. All I remember after thirty years of searching for you.

CON.: NOW do you believe me?

MAG.: Why should I? All that story did was make me homesick for mi tierra!

CON.: Let's go make some chicken mole. That always helps. *(THEY go.)*

EMILY: What will you do, now? Keep going door to door, sharpening the knives of strangers?

JOE: I'm leaving this country altogether, now that the war is over, I'm going down to the Islands like I always wanted.

EMILY: I am my own woman, and my husband's. That is unthinkable.

JOE: What is unthinkable is not that, but the thought of you wasting away here in this shadow of a life. Come. Reclaim yourself with me.

EMILY: You are such a mad fool! Where would we go? Traveling through a land that hates us both?

JOE: I got it all planned out. We'll book passage on a freighter headed down the Atlantic coast, traveling as servant and mistress, till we get to the Islands; I got plenty money saved up. There we can at last be together and be free.

EMILY: Poor Joe. Don't you know that slavery plagues these lands much like our own national sickness?

JOE: Not where we're bound to. A fabulous, free black African Island in the middle of the Colonial sea!

EMILY: Where is this paradise?

JOE: Beautiful Haiti! Free for almost a hundred years, Uncle Sam wouldn't dare put his hands on Haiti!

EMILY: But what of my good name? What of my husband?

MAN OFFSTAGE: Emily! Come in here woman, and help me clean out my earwax!!

EMILY: I'll come with you, Joe. It couldn't be any worse than Philadelphia... *(COMPANY enters for FINALE and curtain call.)*

SONG: *(Tune of "O Sam Houston")*

ALL: *(Sing)* Vaya con Dios, my darling! Adios, so long, fare thee well!

JOE: *(Sings)* Stay by my side in my memory...

EMILY: (Sings) Or stay at my four star hotel!

ALL *(Sing)*
Thank you Emily Morgan, for telling your story to me,
You gave us a true understanding
Of what it means when we fight to be free!

(Lights dim to out)

THE END

Left to right: SkudR Jones and Rita Crosby.
Photo by Rick Malone.

The Living Graves

Stories from the Powder Hill Cemeteries

Note: As You Read *The Living Graves* . . .

The Living Graves, like most of Sterling Houston's plays, is an eclectic blend of post-modern theatricality. From the graveyard setting with intermittent ghost dances and songs to the voice overs identifying names on tombs to the film projections of faces and grave-stones, this historical drama (or spirited documentary) simmers with images of those long dead remembering triumphs and disasters. The spirit of Clara Driscoll, a white property owner, is the main narrator serving as tour guide through the Powder Hill Cemeteries and thus stories of the inhabitants. The drama highlights the lives of a medley of Texas historical figures including Adina DeZavala, a member of the Daughters of the Revolution, Samuel Maverick, a white business-man, politician, land speculator, and cattle baron, General Martin Perfecto De Cos, General Santa Anna's brother-in-law, Mr. Charlie Bellinger, a black politician and entrepreneur, and a hosts of bar types and townspeople.

As one of Houston's characters says, he presents "the good and great as well as the greatly wicked—side by side as when they lived." The mostly didactic tale evolves with conflict as they dispute the interpretations of the past and are caught up in the past clashes in their colorful histories. The characters rise, as if falling, to tell their stories to keep them alive in memory and history.

The narrative, fifteen scenes beginning with the grave diggers prologue, is a combination of presentational style direct address to the audience and representational style character dialogue and action spanning over a hundred years of Texas history.

Production Notes

The Living Graves was first produced in 2005 by Jump-Start Performance Co. in San Antonio, Texas at the Little Carver Theatre. Jump-Start, the Carver Cultural Center, and the Renaissance Guild collaborated to bring it to the stage. The City of San Antonio commissioned the work as part of a project to highlight the history of the city cemeteries. The original cast was as follows:

Grave Digger, Jack Harris, General Cos, Man	Billy Muñoz
Grave Digger, Ben Thompson, Charlie Bellinger, Jody, Man	SkudR Jones
Samuel Maverick Sr., Henchman, Man, Voice	Bill Martin
Clara Driscoll, Mary Ann Maverick, Voice	Rita Crosby
Adina DeZavala, Woman, Voice	Pamela Dean Kenney
Dora, Trixie, Woman	Danielle King
Voices of Townspeople, Friends, DRT, etc.	Sterling Houston Barbara Jones George Spelvin Chuck Squier Lisa Suarez

Directed by Steve Bailey

Characters

Grave Diggers

Clara Driscoll

Adina DeZavala

Samuel A. Maverick

Mary Ann Maverick

General Martin Perfecto de Cos

Jack Harris

Ben Thomson

Dora/Trixie

Mr. Charlie Bellinger

Jody

Voices of Townspeople, Friends of DRT, etc.

Setting

Place: San Antonio, Texas

Time: Prologue, present; flashback to the past 150-160 years
         in memories

Prologue

(Two Gravediggers with shovels prepare a plot for burial)

1st GRAVE DIGGER: *(Sings.)* The toe bone connected to the foot bone, the foot bone connected to the anklebone, the anklebone connected to the leg bone, now hear the word of the Lord ... Whew! This is sure some hard-ass work!

2nd GRAVE DIGGER: It helps when you sing, don't it. Hard work is good for you. Puts hair on your chest. *(Continues song together)* The leg bone connected to the knee bone, the knee bone connected to the thigh bone, Thigh bone connected to the backbone, the back bone connected to the shoulder bone. Don't stop singing ...

1st GRAVE DIGGER: I can't remember what's connected to the shoulder bone.

2nd GRAVE DIGGER: The neck bone and then the head bone! I already told you yesterday.

1st GRAVE DIGGER: I don't know why we didn't use the backhoe. It's much faster, you know?

2nd GRAVE DIGGER: Yeah we coulda, but sometimes you need to know the old fashioned ways before going on to something easier. You know?

1st GRAVE DIGGER: Yeah, I guess. I know my arms are killing me.

2nd GRAVE DIGGER: Do what you can. It's getting dark fast, guess we can finish up in the morning.

1st GRAVE DIGGER: Good. *(Sound of distant voices)* Hey! Do you hear that?

2nd GRAVE DIGGER: Hear what? My hearing ain't what it used to be.

1st GRAVE DIGGER: Voices, it's weird. *(Sings)* neck bone connected to the rib ... bone. You can't hear that?

(Recorded voices: heard and fade under until transition to Clara.)

Thomas Lawson-born in Scotland 1851, died May 3, 1887.

In memory of Ann, wife of Philip Johns, born in Cardiff, Wales, died in San Antonio, 1883.

Carl Lieck, geb in Bremmen, Feb. 1829, gest, Dec. 1869.

Francisca Lopez, our beloved, died Dec. 25, 1929.

Hugh R. Lucas Jr. born 1858, died 1883.

Filemon Martinez, nacio November 1927, fallecio 1932.

Robert Lemuel Morris, born in Dickenson Co. Tenn., 1831, died in San Antonio, 1866.

Lizzie, beloved wife of Rufus S. Stedman, born 1836, died 1882.

Aurora Roduges, died April 19, 1920, age 2 months, 15 days.

Austin Romine, 1910, died 1942.

Louise Schuetze, born, Dessau, Germany, geboren 1799, gestorben 1878.

Richard O. Toscano 1860-1936.

Eugene J. Toscano, our darling, 1936-1939.

In memory of H. Voelcker, born 1815 in Rostock Meckleburg, Germany died June 1871.

Sacred to the memory of Walter F. Watson who departed this life in Feb1883, and his wife Frederica D. Watson who departed this life March, 1883.

Erected by the Tomas Chalmers to the memory of his brother, born at Baglie, Dron Parish, Bertshire, Scotland, died April 1879.

In memory of William Crouch Davies, Lient. Col. of the Austrian and U.S. Army, born Lambeth England Mar. 1823, died Sept. 1882.

In memory of Dr. Fred G.B. Hasenburg–born in Dassel Germany 1934, died in Austin Texas, 1874.

H.B. Stumberg, Nov. 1818 – Mar. 1887.

Eduard Elmondorf - geb den 4th Marz, 1821 in Wesel. Preuszen, gest den Marz 1865.

In San Antonio, Texas - F.W. McAllister 1856-1907.

In memory of W.A. Menger, born in Windeken Germany, Mar. 1827-died Mar. 1871.

Carl Gross geb den Nov. 1830, gest den Feb. 1893.

Edward Steves, Jr.-Nov. 1858, Nov. 1908.

Our Beloved Pastor Rev. John W Neil D.D. Pastor of First Presbyterian Church, born, Portsmouth Virginia, Feb. 1837, died April, 1891.

Josephine Houston Frost, 1853-1921.

Thomas Grayson Lubbock – June 1868-April 1889.

Peter Hoefgen, 1823-1896.

Charles A. Wurzbach, Born Mannheim Germany, Nov. 1835—died Aug. 1892.

Christopher Upson, Luet. Col Army of Northern Virginia, Confederate States Army- Oct. 1829, Feb, 1902.

2nd GRAVE DIGGER: *(Spoken over voices)* Well maybe I can. Sometimes strange things happen here when the sun goes down and before the moon comes up.

1st GRAVE DIGGER: Yeah? What kind of things?

2nd GRAVE DIGGER: Let's get our tools together and go on home. The daytime is for the living . . . The night belongs to . . . them.

1st GRAVE DIGGER: Them? You're making me nervous now, hombre.

2nd GRAVE DIGGER: I've heard stories that if you're in this grave-yard after dark, in the moonlight, well, strange sounds and sights are pretty commonplace . . .

1st GRAVE DIGGER: *(Pause.)* You ever see anything . . . strange?

2nd GRAVE DIGGER: Me? No, son, not really. I ain't that brave.

1st GRAVE DIGGER: Me neither, dude . . . Let's go!

2nd GRAVE DIGGER: I'm ready.

(Gravediggers exit with their tools, etc. as the music swells and the sky grows darker. Voices continue.)

Scene 1

(Dora, Adina, Maverick, Jody, Clara and Jack assemble to tell their stories.)

(Film projected of players in a tight cluster. They move slowly in a circle and are seen from above, looking up. Their faces are in full view.)

DORA: Where are we?

ADINA: I was sleeping so good.

MAVERICK: Why was our sacred peace disturbed so rudely? Why?

JODY: Where the hell are we going?

CLARA: I don't understand, but please have faith. All is well, all is well . . . Oh!

JACK: Who is here? Who be you? Who be me?

ADINA: We seem to be falling in an out-of-control freight elevator, but going down, not up. Down! Down!

DORA: The elevator hasn't even been invented yet--don't be foolish.

CLARA: But yes, it has. After your time it was . . . my goodness!

MAVERICK: I don't like this. I'm feeling dizzy.

JACK: I'm downright scared now.

JODY: Should we pray? Have mercy, have mercy!

ADINA: We're slowing down . . . Can you feel it?

JACK: It's light. I see some light!

DORA: I don't like this. I want to go back to my peace!

CLARA: We are stopping now. Let's go. People are waiting. We need to tell it once more.

JODY: But why?

ADINA: Because it has been forgotten.

MAVERICK: Well, hell, let's go do it then, one more time.

(Video projection of gravestones appears. Music up. Ghosts appear and do a lively stylized square dance. All cast but Clara. At end of the dance, Clara appears from the doors of her projected mausoleum. She is dressed in high 1920s style—gloves and hat. Ghosts exit. She wanders a bit in the shafts of light, and then looks out at audience.)

CLARA: Hello and welcome, one and all, to our special sunset tour. I am Mrs. Driscoll, and I will be your docent today to guide us through the monuments and tombs of this beautiful graveyard. So nice to see so many of you. It isn't a very popular fad these days; to cherish one's forbearers! The land on which we stand was once an active limestone quarry. It was granted to the city of San Antonio by the King of Spain in 1733, and for many years it was used as a site to store gun power, located as it was outside the city limits, and far from any house or farm. Locals referred to it as Powder House Hill.

MAN: Why was we storing powder? Was a war coming or something?

CLARA: Well, yes in fact there was, but that's not why. You see, there was always a need to blast something, a hillside, a river--to make way for building and such.

LADY: Unh huh. Okay.

CLARA: It was not until the 1850s that this land was consecrated as a living graveyard. It was then officially designated as City Cemetery Number One, or Powder Hill. It is so very beautiful here, don't you agree? It's more like a garden than a bone-yard. Not desolate, not frightening like less thoughtful resting places. Ah! These very southern giant live oaks filtering the light down onto the magnificent white marbles, made richer and more beautiful with age, the grand carved pink and gray granites, the carved angles, draped urns and praying hands. Some carved by world famous sculptors like Pompeo Coppini. A tomb is the final evidence of life lived. The stature and significance of the departed is often indicated by the elaborateness of the memorial, although as we shall see, not always. Any questions so far? Good. Here lie the earthly remains of members of a community long gone. They and I have invented a modern city; we molded it from wet caliche, black dirt, limestone and the power of the human will. Do not be for a minute distressed by the fact that I too am passed away. Who better to guide us through this maze to meet the good and great as well as the greatly wicked--side by side as when they lived. In truth, as you must know by now, many of the wicked have hearts of purest gold and the so-called good have only learned to keep their wickedness hidden.

MAN: You ought to know, missy.

CLARA: Yes, well . . . Over there is my little mausoleum. Darling, isn't it. I'm not really in there as you can see; it just sort of represents my story. You see, I was . . . oh, no it wouldn't be polite to start with my own tale, although it is quite a story as you shall see, but good manners and grace are more important now than ever . . . Let me show you something really wonderful. *(Moves over stage left to Maverick monument)* This is the marker for the Maverick clan, a big brood of many generations who made their fortune in San Antonio and in the wider world. The Patriarch Samuel Augustus Maverick lies here, under those columns alongside his beloved Mary Ann. Whether in cattle ranching or politics, no single family had a greater impact on what we have come to know and love as Texas . . .

Scene 2

DINA: Hello. My name is Adina de Zavala. I must sneak in here to tell you a few things about the almighty Mrs. Clara Driscoll. Clara Driscoll, Clara Driscoll, Clara Driscoll. Always Clara, Clara, Clara! First of all she is not a San Antonian but hails from the capital city of Austin by way of Corpus Christi. It really gets on my nerves. She is no saint, but rather a bit of a wild woman, if I may be so bold, way more acquainted with John Barleycorn than John Quincy Adams, if you get my drift. Oh yes. However, Clara was also my beloved sister in the spirit, an inspiration, and the dearest friend I have ever known. But this "savior of The Alamo" business? Nonsense. Everybody must know that I am the real savior, being the granddaughter of Lorenzo De Zavala, the first vice president of the Republic of Texas, and signer of the Republic's Declaration of Independence. Not to mention I am the founder of the De Zavala chapter of the Daughters of the Republic of Texas. My remains are buried in St. Mary's Cemetery, a stone throw from here. It's very modest though very beautiful; you should see it sometime. It is true that Clara wrote the check to acquire the Alamo property thus saving it from demolition. Mrs. Clara Driscoll is no villainess, and I detect no malice in her heart. But over this Alamo business, she simply did not show good judgment . . .

(Lights on Maverick, as he does business as music continues)

Scene 3

MAVERICK: Am I confused, misinformed, or downright delusional? I could'a swore that this first section was mine to tell of me and the progeny that my esteemed family has produced through the several generations, but instead . . . Here we go again jawing about the Alamo! The Alamo! The Alamo! The Alamo! Remember the Alamo! Yes, I remember it alright, no doubt. Those thirteen days of so-called glory that supports our local and national zeitgeist. Hell, none of them adventuring mercenaries was even from Texas except the Mexican Tejanos! They just needed an excuse to justify the doctrine of Manifest Destiny. The hell with 'em all! We wanted to be engaged in the serious business of building a future here! For the future of business . . . It's a little embarrassing to talk about this to all you modern people of today, but you see, this was slavery time. A time when human beings held in bondage were forced to work for nothing or die. Slaves were essential to the economic well being of the nation and in the land of Texas. More than a few folks wanted Texas to be a slave state, although Mexico had outlawed that nasty custom years before.

(Jody appears. He is the servant/slave to Maverick family.)

JODY: Old man Maverick was about as fair and generous as any white man one would likely to come across in those times. He was as good as his word and possessed of a long memory. I remembered how he, a slaveholder himself, refused to take part in that big lynching. Slavery in Texas was kinda different than in the old South. But not different enough. Round here, wasn't no big plantations, and we worked mostly as drivers, smithies, barbers, household help. Some were craftsmen and women, tailors, bakers, stonecutters. Most had some free time to themselves. Yes, I been free and I been slaved and I'm here to tell you; free is better.

MAVERICK: But in a very real sense, enslaved people saved my life, and my wife and child; there wouldn't no Mavericks if not for them.

CLARA: Now Mr. Maverick, lets not exaggerate . . .

DORA: He don't be exaggerating . . . I know you remember that council house fight! Comanches invaded my kitchen looking to assassinate you and baby Sammy. I had to beat them off with a big iron spoon. Bastards!

MAVERICK: The less said about that the better.

DORA: Well hell, it's the damn truth!

MAVERICK: Earlier in that decade, while coming through the wilderness of Alabama from my wife' family home in Tuscaloosa, we were put upon by a band of Cherokee Indian braves; guess they though there were quite enough of us invading their country, so they did their level best to slay us all. But thanks be to providence and the courageous people with us who had been so loyal and true, although enslaved, we managed to fight them off without a single casualty-- wife Mary Ann, baby Sam junior, and I. Our wagon made it through without further incident. When we arrived in San Antonio in 1838, it was still a province ruled by the Republic of Mexico under the authority of General Cos, who as everybody knows, was General Santanna's brother-in-law. Before I knew anything, a group of Anglo immigrants decided to have a little revolution. Wanted to overthrow the Mexicans and steal Texas for themselves. I was arrested by the good general and thrown into jail for the crime of being a white man and suspected revolutionary spy. Wife and servants had to fend for themselves. San Antonio was still the largest and western most city before you came to the great southwestern desert, if you could call a wide place in the road an actual city. It was an odd mixture of Texas revolutionary dreamers, land speculators, native Mexicans and a few hundred Negroes enslaved and free born, caught between the South and the

West. The future was bright and promised much to a citizen with only the slightest ambition. San Antonio quickly gained the reputation of being wide open. Through all of this, the peril and the joy, I had beside me my beloved Mary Ann, *(GENERAL COS in light)* a woman of extraordinary courage and patience. My story is her story as well.

GENERAL COS: Espéreme por favor, wait a minute and hold the phone--though it hasn't been invented yet. Oh. You did not know that the dead are privileged to see both past and future at the same moment, back and forth through time. Oh forgive me please; perhaps you did not know this. The point is, I, General Martin Perfecto de Cos, was supreme ruler of San Antonio de Bejar with the full backing of his Excellency Antonio Lopez de Santa Anna and the power of the awesome Republic of Mexico, which like all nations, has the absolute right to defend its territory. The Americanos called my brother-in-law cruel, a ruthless mean and nasty tyrant. But understand, being a good dictator is a very tricky business. In truth all lands are the property of the Almighty, but down here in Tejas, his Excellency is God's real estate agent.

CLARA: General Cos, con su permiso, I can't allow you to interrupt our proceedings with this apologist propaganda. We all know of the ruthlessness and tyranny of the Mexican rulers . . . I've studied Texas history!

GENERAL COS: Yes, I know, you partially invented it, verdad? So, if somebody comes into your village and asks permission to stay the night and you give permission, you welcome them, and then you wake up in the morning to find your guest has changed the locks and stolen the gold fillings from the teeth of your ancestors, tell me, what would you do? Exactamente.

CLARA: Nevertheless . . . if I may continue.

GENERAL COS: Basta! If I may continue . . . As for the slanderous chisme that I came by my promotion to governor general because of the nagging ways of his Excellency's sister it is a lie! I worked my way up through the ranks for many years. Eventually my dash and heroic charm caught the eye of his excellency's sister who in fact is my dear corozon mi esposa la Doña Maria Elena Conchita. One must use all the tools that the Almighty provides, que no. By the authority of my rank, it is therefore my sovereign duty to suppress rebellions, subdue uprisings, and in general quell all dissent. Which brings us to why I had no choice but to arrest this Maverick fellow. Que huevos. Isn't a Maverick some sort of cow?

CLARA: Moving right along . . . Sam Maverick was a cultured gentleman. One evening he and his wife Mary Ann went to see a play at the Casino Club, it was the tragedy King Lear, and afterward . . .

(Cross fade to Mary and Maverick)

MARY: You're awfully quiet this evening, Samuel.

MAVERICK: Am I?

MARY: Did the play disturb you?

MAVERICK: It was so well performed, that I got somewhat lost in it. Not easy to watch the display of parents and children slaughtering each other to obtain wealth and power, even when stated with such magnificent language.

MARY: Ah yes, one of Mr. Shakespeare's favorite themes. Samuel? Do you mind if we walk back to the house. It's been a while since I've strolled through the plaza.

MAVERICK: Not at all. It's a beautiful night for walking. Granville, take the buggy back to the house, and we shall meet you there directly.

MARY: Seeing children taken by greed and misplaced ambition, even in a play does make me angry. Four of our little darlings were called back to the Lord before they were six years old. It must be accepted with grace.

MAVERICK: Is your grief very bitter?

MARY: No mother should have to witness the death of her child. It is surely one of the greatest burdens anyone can bare. We will all be together in the great by and by. I just thank God for those who survive. A mother could not ask for more loving loyal children . . .

MAVERICK: Our precious little ones.

MARY: Sam, I hope you are able to slow down a bit, now that you have accomplished so much.

MAVERICK: Plenty of time for slowing down in the hereafter, my dear.

MARY: No, I mean it darling. Who else has been so prominent in the founding of the Republic of Texas, The War Between the States, been mayor, senator and a leader of men of destiny? Now you have founded a bank to hold all the wealth you have accumulated through your efforts with cattle and land. Slow down, Sam, please? You can write that book you've always talked about. I can help you.

MAVERICK: It would be wonderful to spend more time with you instead of running all over creation.

MARY: Wouldn't it be nice?

MAVERICK: Look around you. See how San Antonio has prospered--in no small part because of our efforts.

MARY: Yes I know, dear.

MAVERICK: I hope you also know that none of this would have come to pass, surviving seven months in Santa Anna's jail, fighting against succession and for an end to slavery, keeping courage after burying so many babies, none would have been possible without the steadfastness of your unconditional love.

MARY: Oh! Did you see that shooting star?

MAVERICK: Yes indeed, I sure did.

MARY: Did you make a wish?

ADINA: Dear sir, you failed to mention that you are that same Samuel Maverick who became a land speculator and cattle baron in east Texas before coming here. *(To audience)* He was famous for leaving his calves unbranded and roaming free for a long time, so any cow without a brand was said to be a Maverick. Get it? The name of course later became shorthand to describe any person who was a rebel or possessed an independent spirit. Later still, the Maverick name was used for a western TV show in the nineteen sixties, and eventually, a mediocre Dallas basketball team.

MAVERICK: Right you are Doña Adina. Thanks for clearing that up. Your sense of history is truly astonishing.

ADINA: But don't get me wrong. Samuel Maverick the elder was no plaster saint. He did not, as the saying goes, suffer fools gladly, and had a temper like a firecracker. Once he pulled a pistol on a poor woman who was trying to contact his departed son in a séance. Must have been quite a sight . . .

(Action sequence)

MARY: Sam please! Put the gun away, husband!

MAVERICK: Is it not enough that I have had to fight off Comanches, thieving outlaws, General Santa Anna's army, reconstruction, carpet-baggers, the Ku Klux Klan, charlatans of every persuasion? Now I'm supposed to tolerate this spiritualist con woman who brings false hope to my long-suffering wife? My little boy is dead. I saw him buried. It's enough to make me pull out my pistol and use it!

DORA: But Miz Mary Ann, she sent for that gypsy woman herself! Now Mr. Sam, remember your heart. You know what your Doctor said.

MAVERICK: I know. I know.

ADINA: Those Mavericks were a gifted clan--extremely adept at breeding strong cattle, as well as breeding many Mavericks.

MAVERICK: Watch it now, Adina . . .

(End of action)

ADINA: Why don't you tell us about that famous Council House fight? You were there were you not?

MAVERICK: I'd really rather not go into that . . . Long time ago. It's dead and buried now.

CLARA: That's exactly why you should speak if it. It's alright, Sam.

MAVERICK: This story still brings me the deepest sorrow. Why I should feel such pain, I can't really say. I don't want to tell you this, but as you suggest, it needs telling. It was a bad dirty business and heart-breaking to witness--The Council House Fight. Felt more like a mas-sacre. It began, you see, when we were in the process of negotiating a prisoner exchange with the Comanche. They'd kidnapped several of our settlers and confined them in the worst conditions-- ill treatment, bad food. They was poor folk like many of us, but that didn't matter; they hated our guts entirely. How can I judge them? Tell me. We met on their land at the Comanche council house, where they did all serious business. We had a handful of their Comanche men, people we had caught raiding or stealing horses and such, and had brought them with us to the council room to set things clear that very day. First thing we learned was that these people had killed all the men prisoners for no good reason except meanness. Our anger grew to rage when they brought in the women, our women, who were scarred and beat up and near broken. They were so pitiful. Some had been raped and forced to bare little Comanche babies. Well, what can I say about it except our white men went crazy and began to shoot and stab every Indian in sight. We managed to get away with those poor ladies and no fatal casualties, but for the next months, a killing spree erupted. No white or Comanche was safe, as this vengeful harassment continued. Enough said I guess. Council House Fight. Not everything in our illustrious past was dressed in glory. No sir.

CLARA: Very sad, but if I may continue with my tour . . .

MAVERICK: Yes, of course. Didn't mean to get so carried away.

ADINA: Yes, yes by all means . . . Please continue. So interesting!

CLARA: Now we come to the rather humble grave of Vaudeville Jack Harris, a real San Antonio story. One of triumph and tragedy. He died after a good life partaking in some of Texas's greatest pastimes, politics, gambling and drinking good whisky. His life ended swiftly with a gunshot through the heart.

Scene 4

(Jack sits at card table with Ben. They are playing Faro, and Jack plays a winning hand. Gathers chips and cash. They play another hand throughout song. Ben loses again, can find no cash, so pulls out a gold pocket watch and chain. Jack scoops it up.)

VOICE: Jack Harris's famous Vaudeville theater presents for your pleasure, direct from Saint Louis Missouri, The Belle of the Bayous, the one and only Miss Trixie Tremain!

TRIXIE: *(Sings)*

> Frankie and Johnnie were lovers
> O Lordy how they did love
> They swore to be true to each other
> Just as true as the stars above
> He was her man but he's doing her wrong
>
> Frankie she was a good woman
> Just as every one knows
> She gave her man a hundred dollars
> Just to buy him a new suit of clothes
> He was her man but he done her wrong
>
> Johnnie went down to the corner
> He asked for a glass of beer
> Frankie went down in an hour or so
> Said has my loving Johnnie been here
> He's my man but he's doing me wrong
>
> I ain't gonna tell you no stories
> I ain't gonna tell you no lies
> I saw your lovin' Johnnie
> Making love to Nellie Bligh
> He's your man but he's doing you wrong
>
> Frankie went home in a hurry
> She didn't go for fun
> She hurried home to get a hold of
> A big bad forty-four gun
> He's her man but he's doing her wrong . . .

(Frankie mimes drawing and aiming gun)

Take that, you dirty dog!

(Drum makes sound of two gunshots. Continues to sing.)

> Roll me over darling, this is what Johnnie said,
> Roll me over slow
> Roll me on my right side
> Cause my left one hurts me so
> He was my man but he was doing me wrong!

(Trixie bows and exits)

JACK: Son you ain't had lady luck on your side today. *(Jack gathers more chips/money and pockets it.)*

BEN: That's why they call it gambling, I reckon.

JACK: I reckon you'll win it all back before too long.

BEN: Yeah, just not today, Jack. You cleaned me out my friend. Shoulda known better than to play Faro, with you.

JACK: What do you mean by that, Ben?

BEN: Everybody knows that Faro is the dealer's game . . . don't they?

JACK: Do they?

TRIXIE: *(Enters in show costume and sits on Jack's lap.)* Hi ya, fellas.

JACK: How's tricks Miss Trixie? *(They kiss.)*

BEN: Well I guess I'll mosey on back to Austin, don't want to miss that last train . . .

JACK: Trixie, this here is my old pal Ben Thompson. We go back a long way, don't we partner?

BEN: Sure. Dang right. We fought the Yankees in that nasty war.

JACK: Yup. Come to Texas around the same time, and joined the forces of law and order.

BEN: Yeah. I was a constable in Austin . . .

JACK: About the same time I went to work with the San Antonio sheriff's department. And we was both of us Texas Rangers! Hotdoggitt!

TRIXIE: Sure enough? And now you run this salon and vaudeville theater on Commerce Street. How lucky can you get?

JACK: Well right. Why live a life of shooting and getting' shot at? Knew I could make a living doing something I loved. Gambling and watching fine women on stage . . . ha ha, right Ben?!

BEN: Right . . . well . . .

JACK: Billy the Kid, John Wesley Hardin, Butch Cassidy, Frank and Jesse, all the big outlaws come in here when they're in town.

BEN: Yeah, I need to get, now. Nice to meet you miss Trixie.

TRIXIE: Adios. Come back soon and catch my show.

BEN: Alright enough, I'll be back, I'm sure of that. Need to win some of the money that you cleaned me out of. Night all.

JACK: Now, Ben, I hope you don't hold no grudge against me, cause you lost. There's been something sticking in your craw for a while, if you ain't man enough to tell me what it is . . . (Ben fingers his gun) that wouldn't be wise.

BEN: What do you mean? Man enough! You got no cause to get insulting. I wouldn't' hold nothing against you, never. Unless I found out you was cheating.

TRIXIE: No, no, everybody knows Jack Harris runs an honest game.

JACK: What? Cheating? Be careful now partner. I think you should stay up there in Austin until you get that crazy notion out of you head . . . my friend.

BEN: I'll be back, my friend, when I'm good and goddamn ready. *(Exits)*

TRIXIE: Months, then years went by with nary a word from old Ben Thompson. Life at the Vaudeville Theater went on pretty much as always. Jack heard the rumors that old Ben had vowed to gun him down, and was determined to be prepared for it. Then early one evening in '82, Jack heard the talk that Ben Thomson was in town looking for him. He sat with a rifle across his lap and waited, so he could greet Ben properly if he should walk in the door. Afternoon had become night and the candlelight and smoke from the cigar smoking men rose and swirled like fog. He watched the door. The piano man was playing that old time song. Jack said good evening tipped his hat to a customer, just as the barrel of a Colt 45 pistol split through them old swinging doors. I guess Ben was ready. Before Jack had a chance to aim and shoot . . .

JACK: Hey Ben! What the hell . . . you son of a bitch!

TRIXIE: That was all he could utter before the bullet from Ben Thomson's Colt revolver pierced his heart. *(Gunshot. JACK falls.)* No more Jack. His obituary said he was the wickedest man in town, but that ain't the truth. He didn't go to church every Sunday, it's a fact. And many of his pals were on the pungent side of unsavory, but he never refused a helping hand to anybody in need. Never broke a promise to nobody. Never hit a woman, except in self-defense. From the sheriff and the mayor to the shoe shine man on the corner. They all knew they could count on Jack Harris.

(Voice overs)

VOICE 1: "Jack, thanks for getting my brother out of jail,"

VOICE 2: "I'm ever so grateful for you keeping my mamma from getting evicted off her land; I am truly."

VOICE 3: "I love my job working over at the flour mill, Mr. Harris. Thanks for putting in a good word."

VOICE 4: "Jack, old buddy, you know I would never would have won the mayor's race without you being behind me."

VOICE 5: "Bless you, Mr. Jack Harris. You ain't no saint, but then everybody ain't."

TRIXIE: Lord his funeral procession was something to behold! Leaving from Soledad with his body laid out in a black and silver hearse, coffin covered with red and white roses. It was followed by carriages, men on horseback, wagons, buggies--people walking wearing black in the midday sun--ladies in carriages wearing hats and veils which didn't hide their tears. When the hearse reached the gate to the cemetery, you could look down Commerce Street and see an unbroken procession of mourners, moving in a stately pace as the bells echoed out from the towers of San Fernando Cathedral and St. Joseph's Church. Everybody wanted to pay last respects to Mr. Jack. I'm telling you that for a fact.

CLARA: And so as I was saying, here lies Mister Jack Harris, gambler, entrepreneur, democratic party chairman, king maker and man of the people, resting in peace a few yards from me. Nice tombstone portrait. *(Visual of grave stone with an oval portrait of Jack wearing his big handlebar moustache. Transition Music--"Frankie & Johnnie.")*

Scene 5

ADINA: There are those still today who assume that the struggle for control of the Alamo was a Mexican versus Anglo situation. This is simply a popular oversimplification, and one that I will now try to clarify. I, Adina de Zavala am not a Mexican woman. Per se. My grandfather Lorenzo married a beauty from the North named Emily West. My father of course had the De Zavala blood in his veins, but my blonde-headed grandmother did not. At best I may define myself as a person of mixed heritage. Comprende?

JODY: Not Mexican, huh, if your grandfather was Mexican, ain't all the blonde hair in the world enough to make you white. Comprende?

DORA: Guess she ain't never heard about the one-drop theory. Huh?

JODY: For real.

DORA: That sure does complicate the mix, now don't it.

BOTH: Passing!

ADINA: I am not Mexican, or so I have been told, but we can all agree indeed, San Antonio is a Mexican city. Then, now and forever. Founded by the Spanish, It became part of northern Mexico you understand, when the first revolution kicked the Spaniards back to Spain. After the fiasco of Maximillano and the French, it became the Mexican Nation. This land has always been part of it, like it or not. In San Antonio we have nearly three-hundred years of fiestas, pachangas, enchiladas, caldo de res, caldo de pollo, chalupas, tacos big and tacos small, and what did the Irish Anglos give us? Or the Germans give us?

MAVERICK: The Anglos I'll not speak of but the Germans, my dear, gave us the finest beer the world has ever known- perfect thing to wash those tamales down.

(Lights change)

Scene 6

(Jody gathers dead flowers from graves and puts them in a trash barrel.)

JODY: Ya'll probably think this is all ancient history, don't you. Well, somebody said, history ain't nothing but the story of the migration of folks moving from one place to another place. Think about it. Old Steven Austin was a pretty slick hombre, see, he wanted white folks to migrate here from the old South, and they wasn't about to move and have to free their people in a free state. Austin and them made sure that things would go in their favor. That's what that revolution was all about, sure enough. Alamo, Goliad, San Jacinta all of it had not a damned thing to do with freedom, but as always about maintaining that peculiar institution. Mr. Maverick was a man of his times, but he saw through the lying. These were mean days. Sad as it is to say, in point of fact, colored folks needed a friendly white man to help him navigate the shark-infested shoals that surrounded us.

(Music transition and lights)

Scene 7

(Streets of San Antonio–1900. Music. Folks rush through streets, using tombs as doorways.)

2nd MAN: They gonna tear it down, this time it's true.

1st MAN: Tear what down?

2nd MAN: The Alamo you danged fool. The danged old Alamo

1st MAN: No foolin'? Where did you get that story from?

2nd MAN: Same place I get all my news! The San Antonio Light, Evening News Bulletin and Tattler.

1st MAN: They'll never tear down that old pile of rocks.

2nd MAN: Wanna bet?

1st MAN: No. Not really.

(Lights up on Maverick)

MAVERICK: Seems' like to me, men'll do the goshdarndest things, work every thing ass-backwards and hind part before, until some smart women come in to the equation, get together and get it right for everybody concerned.

Scene 8

CLARA: Are you all enjoying our little journey back in time? Any one have a question or concern?

MAN: Yeah. I'm getting real hungry. How long before we go home?

CLARA: Not very long, sir. We are nearly half way through the high points.

WOMAN: I have a question. Why aren't there more Mexicans in this graveyard?

CLARA: No, there are a few, very few. Oh dear, well you see, for all its greatness, the United States of America is still a rigidly segregated nation. It is the law. But more importantly the Mexicanos, like the Coloreds and the Jews have their own cemeteries. People just prefer to be with their own kind. It's human nature.

WOMAN: Oh I see . . .

CLARA: But before we go on with our little tour, I must pause and re-live an episode that will give you a new understanding of hunger; it may explain much about my own history and the history of the legendary Alamo.

MAN: Great! I'll get my coon-skin hat!

WOMAN: Will you just hush.

Scene 9

(1918)

CLARA: Isn't it wonderful Adina! Another parcel of antique artifacts donated for the restoration of the Alamo. Here's a candlestick from a family in Ohio, whose great granddaddy found it on the chapel floor, and this crucifix and rosary beads, from California. Look! A cooking pot that might have been used by the heroes themselves, a knife fork and spoon.

ADINA: Looks like real silver, too!

CLARA: These items are a fine addition to our collection for the Alamo museum. Once it is brought back to standard, we can furnish it with actual goods from the day of defeat.

ADINA: Yes, indeed. A real treasury. What a blessing.

CLARA: Let's lock them in the old chapel for safekeeping.

ADINA: A fine idea, no one will expect to find things of value in that old ruin.

CLARA: Help me carry this stuff, if you will. Oh, I must be off for a lunch with the mayor and his wife. Will you lock it in and close the padlock? Make sure you do. *(Exits)*

ADINA: Of course, I will, I am our history's custodian as much as anybody. Adios Clara. *(After Clara goes, Adina drags the bundle of loot into the gates of the long barracks, and locks it.)* There they will be safe. After all, I am the granddaughter of Lorenzo DeZavala, the first vice president of the Republic of Texas. Therefore, the righteous guardian of the legacy of our history. I will do whatever it takes to protect and preserve that legacy, until the day I die!

Scene 10

(Days later. ADINA gavels for order, scene is played in silhouette with the men filling in with fans and big feathered hats.)

ADINA: Ladies, please come to order quickly! Thank you. This afternoon I bring you an announcement off stupendous moment that rivals that day when we first received our charter. I think it only fair the person most responsible be given the honor of making the announcement-- Mrs. Clara Driscoll. *(Applause)*

CLARA: Ladies, we have fought long and hard for the goal we have today achieved. I'm proud and thrilled to announce that the Hugo

Schmeltzer Company's deal with the U.S. Army has collapsed and the Alamo property has been taken of the market. In negotiations with the owners, I grew weary of the wrangling manipulations. So I just went into my purse took out my checkbook and paid the asking price $75,000. So now it's ours, ladies. The Alamo is ours! Here's the keys and deed to the property. I think that calls for a toast! *(Cheers and applause. Champagne and glasses.)* Let's drink a toast to the power of historic preservation!

DORA: Careful now Mrs. Clara, You know how you get with a little firewater in you. Just have one sip!

CLARA: Who are you?

DORA: You may not remember me, but oh yes indeed. I know you. I used to work for you. Washing, cleaning and a little cooking, though you always said I couldn't cook. I have had to take your shoes off on more that one occasion to tuck you in after too much celebrating. Who am I? My name ain't that important, you could never seem to remember it no how. It's Dora, or to folks like you, Miss Dora. My grave is over yonder, in the colored section of course, on the corner of Montana Street and New Braunfels Avenue. Yeah, the one with no fence and no grand gravestones. Segregation! Separate and unequal even after death. That's another story, honey . . .

ADINA: Take your seat please. You are out of order. Let me see that. *(Takes deed and reads.)* Ah just as I thought the Hugo & Schmeltzer property is deeded in trust not to you personally Clara dear, but to the Daughters and to me as founder of the DeZavala chapter, if I'm not mistaken.

CLARA: I don't think that's quite right, but I suppose . . .

ADINA: Excellent! Then may I have the keys, if you don't mind? I would like to asses the condition of our newly acquired holdings, that is, if no one objects . . .

CLARA: *(Produces large key ring)* As you know, these keys go to the front and back of the chapel, and the gates of the long barracks which will soon be demolished to make room for a garden and gazebo. Then we will refurbish the chapel and . . .

ADINA: *(Grabs ring)* What? Wait a momentito, I never agreed on any such thing, and never will. *(The women engage in slapstick tug of war.)* The Long Barracks is where the actual battle took place . . . not that broken down old chapel!

CLARA: But Adina my dear, you were voted down! The chapel is the key to our future! It is an icon in the making! We'll print thousands of cards with a picture of the façade and caption it "The Shrine of Texas Liberty!"

ADINA: But you know, as do we all, that there was no fighting, no sacrifice, no drama, no blood and guts in the chapel. Jim Bowie never set foot in it!

DORA: Jim Bowie was the biggest slave trader in Texas, you know.

CLARA: You just don't understand marketing and mass promotion, and no doubt ever will.

ADINA: Perhaps, but I understand history and truth! *(Adina wins tug and holds keys above her head. She backs into 'gates' of Long Barracks.)* I will lock myself in the real Alamo until you come to your senses, Clara Driscoll! *(She goes in.)*

CLARA: We shall see . . . Ask the sheriff to post a guard at the barracks gate. He must forbid anyone to bring Miss Adina food or water, day or night. How dare you defy me, Dina, how DARE you! We'll see how long her hunger strike lasts. Ha! *(Women exit)*

Scene 11

(Later that night)

ADINA: It's rather chilly in here. I hope I don't catch cold, or worse. Sometimes it becomes necessary to place principle above personal comfort. I am, as you know the granddaughter of Lorenzo de Zavala the first vice-president of the independent Texas Republic. He served at the side of Sam Houston himself. That same heroic blood still flows in my veins. Oh, I have had many suitors make no mistake. But I have chosen to sacrifice the comforts of husband and family to devote my life entirely to the cause for which my ancestors died. I will remain here until Clara and the others come to their senses and do the proper historically authentic thing. I do wish I had prepared a little better for this self-imposed exile. But I doubt that the good citizens of San Antonio will let me starve or die of thirst . . . I hope.

Scene 12

CLARA: Adina insists on being so melodramatic, trying to get sympathy for her lost cause. Hump! I, in the name of the Daughters of the Republic of Texas have petitioned the state to charter a new chapter of the DRT, one that doesn't include Miss DeZavala and her gang. Furthermore, I have locked the gate from the outside. Ha! She called for a hunger strike. Let's see how hungry she gets before begging to get out.

ADINA: This is monstrous! Will no one show me any mercy? Clara Driscoll, you were my best friend, my best . . . *(She sobs)*

(An armed guard stands at gate. Night falls and guard yawns and falls asleep. Man approaches and calls out whisper)

MAN: Adina! Adina!

ADINA: *(Adina comes forward)* Who calls for me? The ghost of Jim Bowie? I won't let you down.

MAN: Miss Adina! Adina De Zavala!

ADINA: Is it my savior at last?

MAN: Come out to the gate. *(She does.)* I have a little cup of coffee and a muffin for you. It may get you through this night. Put your mouth against this knothole crack, that's right. Here I will pour you a little water and coffee. Don't spill it, Miss.

ADINA: Alright . . . *(Adina does as directed.)* Thank you friend, you have saved my poor life. Tell Mrs. Driscoll that after these three days, I am more determined than ever. And ask her about the time she was nearly arrested for being drunk and disorderly at the White Plaza Hotel. She wasn't so high and mighty then. Just high! I will never surrender. As long as I have the blood of . . . Dear God, Here they come!

(Enter Clara and henchmen)

MAN: We have here a court order for you ma'am, to hand over the deeds all stolen artifacts and all keys to the Alamo property to the custody of the representatives of the Governor of Texas where they will be held for arbitration. Knock it down boys. *(They sledgehammer the gate. It opens. After a moment Adina appears.)*

JODY: And so it was. The truly historic Long Barracks was demolished without so much as a fare thee well. After arbitration and lawsuits back and forth, the old chapel was spruced up and advertised in the press. The myth of the Alamo heroes was invented and quickly became history. Tourists came first in a trickle, and then as a flood.

CLARA: Let's have a snort to celebrate!

DORA: Watch it now, Mrs. Clara . . . !

CLARA: You again. Who in the world are you? Oh never mind.

ADINA: As for me, I took my defeat with grace. Yes, I surrendered the artifacts, and returned the keys. I content myself with the knowledge that I am on the side of historic accuracy, and many others agree with me, powerless though we may be to change anything. Time, as it always does, will, as they say, tell. I continued to work for the preservation of our legacy, saved the humble adobe that had been General Cos's little house, and the grand stucco Spanish style Villa Navarro, which was the Royal Spanish Governor's mansion long before any one had ever heard of Steven Austin. I never understood how Clara could betray me. I never did. She didn't apologize ever, thought she had won the battle. She was my best friend, you know. People forget.

CLARA: I always felt somewhat sorry for Adina. She never knew it, yes, I saw to that. I heard she was doing fine, had her fortune, respect. Never saw her again. We had been such good friends, such believers in the great work of preservation. It was a golden time. I'll never understand why she betrayed me that way, so publicly . . . how things between us became so cold. After all these years I still don't.

ADINA: Clara and I never spoke to each other again. I caught a glimpse of her one day in McAllister's store, but she turned away averting her eyes. At least, I think it was her. I lived out my life in a modest penthouse atop Mr. Menger's charming hotel, a stone's throw from the Alamo enterprise. There I could watch the people come and go—saints and traitors alike. I am certain that among all people who love the truth, I will never be forgotten. *(She crosses and during the following goes up to the "balcony" of the Menger.)*

Scene 13

MAVERICK: Fine. At least, that's the way the tabloids told it. Others have a different memory. Adina DeZavala was nobody's fool. Yes she was locked in, but held the key to her liberation at all times. Despite what Mrs. Driscoll thought about Dina's ability to understand PR, she knew that a little martyrdom went a long way to garner public sympathy; she let it grow into a national story. It was picked up as far as the New York Times. Hell, she didn't even drink coffee. Can we move on now . . . ?

DORA: Finally!

JODY: At long last!

CLARA: Of course. I merely thought that it was important to go into some detail about this history. Moving on . . . Here is the monument to a former mayor a dynamic politician and business man Mr. King Bryan Callahan, *(Visual of 'robber baron' with whiskers and big cigar)* An important mayor, power broker, influence peddler and politico who held forth picking candidates, rigging votes buying influence in Austin and Washington D.C. until he died of corruption in the middle of a dirty land deal with unscrupulous speculators. His son, Big Junior King Callahan, took over the empire with even more zeal and ruthlessness than his daddy. There was a Callahan in the mayor's office for nearly one hundred years. Junior was re-elected nine times. Where were term limits when we really needed them? Eventually the Mavericks came to consolidate power and gave birth to fusion politics . . . !

MAVERICK: What she's talking about is the fact that we Mavericks, my boy Sam the Second, especially, cleverly united the Mexicans and Negroes and labor with visionary white progressives into a voting block to break the back of the political machine that had run San Antonio for decades.

JODY: A real coalition you might say.

MAVERICK: Hell, we just got sick and tired of political patronages, old boy favoritism and the stench of cheap cigars. It was time for change and we sure enough changed it all.

JODY: Not many colored folks voted in them days. Between the lynching and the slow progress since emancipation, we just thought it was a waste of time. Then too, there was the poll tax. Some folks called it the 'polecat tax' cause it did surely stink. It was like you had to pay a fee to get your constitutional right to vote. This was a common ploy throughout the South to suppress our voices. Most didn't bother to participate at all.

DORA: Along came Mr. Sam Maverick Jr. who befriended the most powerful man in the colored community, Mr. Charlie Bellinger. He organized all the Negro preachers, high rolling gamblers, school teachers maids and cooks and such, to work together with the Mexicans and rebel whites. Bellinger was much loved though he was a gambler and bootlegger himself. He was rich. It was rare for a colored man to have any money, so nobody passed judgment on how he acquired it.

JODY: He sure did have it though. Got the streets paved on the East side,

DORA: So colored churchgoers wouldn't have to track mud into Rev. So and So's church on a rainy day . . .

JODY: . . . built a fire station on our side of town—

DORA: . . . so that help had a chance of reaching a burning building before it got reduced to ashes waiting for the North Side Brigade.

JODY: Opened a clinic where colored doctors and nurses cared for colored patients . . .

DORA: Opened a dentist office . . .

JODY: Founded a library, funded by a grant from Mr. Andrew Carnegie . . .

DORA: Founded a newspaper and even organized a Negro League baseball team!

JODY: Then lo and behold, in a little while, Mr. Maverick who was cleverly promoting all this change was elected Mayor of San Antonio!

Scene 14

BELLINGER: The basic problem with the Negro is we are afraid to use our own self-evident power. In my view, behind every man, great or humble, black or white there is a colored woman, keeping things proper and in good order. Cooking, cleaning, having babies, taking care of same, making a comfortable home, and planting a proper garden.

ADINA: Nobody can argue with that. Also planning, dreaming, strategizing bypassing the Jim Crow dictates of conventional wisdom in order to lay the groundwork for our prosperous future.

DORA: We were sure 'nuff busy, but what were we supposed to do? Couldn't vote, or openly take part in civic activities; most couldn't read nor write. And they deprived us of our basic rights till the nineteen twenties. Even the great Miss Susan B. Anthony fought for the vote for white women and colored men, leaving us black ladies out of the equation.

BELLINGER: But still, colored ladies where the backbone of their community. Our struggles would have been far more difficult without their full participation. Those gallant ladies had influence in many households colored and white, and through churches and civic clubs knitted together the fabric of the Negro population. How did we manage to do all this? It wasn't no accident, you can believe that.

(Video of Bellinger portrait, black life etc.)

DORA: Dear Mr. Bellinger,
I'm writing to you in response to your help and support for our school. We will use a large part of your contribution to purchase books from the book depository. True, these books are outdated and well used. But will go far to assist our students to develop reading skills, and open up the wider world to them.

BELLINGER: Dear Sirs:
I have considered the proposal you presented to me vis-à-vis the development and construction of an office building in the downtown area. I believe this proposition is very feasible and essential to the progress of our city.

DORA: Mr. Charlie Bellinger:

Our girls and I have made you this little valentine to express their gratitude and mine for your support. We had a fine time at Camp Elvira, and were able to practice wilderness skills as well as re-enforce our community values, leadership, physical exercise camaraderie, and cheerfulness.

BELLINGER: Sirs:

Your letter of the 19th in response to my offer of financial support was disturbing and somewhat insulting. For me, with my considerable philanthropic efforts, to be diminished, to be kept hidden under an agreement to operate as a silent partner, so as not to embarrass your consortium, because of my color, this sirs fills me with rage.

DORA: Mr. Bellinger:

I am so happy to have you helping us out. The young colored men in our city have precious little to look forward too, given the continuing obstacles placed in our path. They are leaving in droves, to explore greener pastures. But you sir, are a living example for them and for all of us, proving that one's fate despite entrenched prejudice is, with the help of the almighty, in one's own hands.

BELLINGER: Sirs:

I am so convinced that this new downtown skyscraper project must go forward. I will therefore swallow my considerable pride, and agree to the proposal you have made. *(Aside)* Lord, how long? How long?!

(Transition music and projection of Driscoll tomb)

Scene 15

(Late evening, long moon shadows) (Chorus of dead, behind scrim in fog)

ALL: *(Speaking together, or in turn.)*
    My father, my mother,
    My cousin, my children,
    My Heart, my freedom,
    My enslaver, my saint,
    My demon, my future,
    My ancient past, my recent past,
    My eternity, my friend,

My hero, my villain,
My truth, my illusion,
My friend, my guide,
My inspiration, my healer,
My scorn, my sickness,
My immortality, my star,
My galaxy, my warrior,
My trust, my faith,
My love, my love, my love, my love, my love, my love . . .

CLARA: Now, before we leave, we will look more closely at my lovely mausoleum. It was inspired by an ancient Greek temple and is made of the finest granite; I think it is grand without being, well, grandiose. It sits here on this little hillside, turning the heads of all who pass. As we come to finish our tour, there are a few things I would like to clarify. I am a published writer, a professional with two novels to my credit as well as a Broadway play. My integrity is not to be questioned by any reasonable person. Also, my wealth and all I accomplished with it was entirely my own money, inherited from my dear Daddy and redoubled by good advice from my husband. And the persistent rumors that I with a group of celebrating ladies were thrown out of the White Plaza Hotel in Corpus Christi for loud and rowdy behavior is . . . true. We were not falling down drunk as the story goes, but they didn't have to be so rude. I promised them that my lady friends and I would someday empty our chamber pots onto the White Plaza roof. My revenge was sweet. I built the Driscoll Hotel next door to the White Plaza, making it taller and grander than all its neighbors. Up on the roof, I had them construct this little extension platform directly over the White Plaza roof and well; I had vowed to piss on them all one day. Clara Driscoll always keeps her word. *(Church bell rings, rooster crows)*

ADINA: What a thrilling story. I'm really quite proud of all we did, proud of myself, and Clara Driscoll too.

CLARA: Ah, the sky is growing light. The dawn approaches and we must conclude our little tour of the Powder House Hill Cemetery also known as City Cemetery Number One. We encourage you to return on your own and explore more deeply the beautiful stones and statues, the resting place of the some of the wonderful people who lived and loved San Antonio and left their mark on us all forever.

DORA: *(From aside)* That's right Miss Driscoll, you tell it till they know it all. *(Yawns.)* Oh, I'm so sleepy . . .

(Voice over of dead softly under . . .)

Louise Schuetze, born, Dessau, Germany, geboren 1799, gestorben 1878.

Richard O. Toscano, 1860-1936.

Eugene J. Toscano, our darling, 1936-1939.

In memory of H. Voelcker, born 1815 in Rostock Meckleburg, Germany died June 1871.

Sacred to the memory of Walter F. Watson who departed this life in Feb. 1883, and his wife Frederica D. Watson who departed this life March 1883.

Erected by the Tomas Chalmers to the memory of his brother, born at Baglie, Dron Parish, Bertshire, Scotland, Died April 1879.

In memory of William Crouch Davies, Late Lient. Col. of the Austrian and U.S. Army, born Lambeth England Mar. 1823, died Sept. 1882.

In memory of Dr. Fred G.B. Hasenburg –born in Dassel Germany 1934, died in Austin Texas, 1874.

H.B. Stumberg, Nov. 1818 – Mar. 1887.

Eduard Elmondorf-geb den 4th Marz, 1821 in Wesel Preuszen, gest den Marz 1865 In San Antonio, Texas.

F.W. McAllister 1856-1907.

In memory of W.A. Menger, born in Windeken Germany, Mar. 1827- died Mar. 1871.

Carl Gross geb den Nov. 1830, gest den Feb. 1893.

Edward Steves, Jr.-Nov. 1858, Nov 1908.

Our Beloved Pastor Rev. John W Neil D.D. Pastor of First Presbyterian Church, born, Portsmouth Virginia, Feb. 1837, died April, 1891.

Josephine Houston Frost, 1853-1921.

Thomas Grayson Lubbock – June 1868-April 1889.

CLARA: In closing I urge you to remember the unseen.

ADINA: Remember Adina De Zavala, pioneer historian, granddaughter of the first vice president of The Republic, and a true savior of the Alamo.

MAVERICK: Remember Samuel senior and junior who brought change and imagination when there was precious little to be had.

DORA: Think of Miss Dora, a living witness to history.

JACK: Remember Jack Harris, gunslinger, democrat and man of the people who died with his boots on.

BELLINGER: Mr. Charlie Bellinger, who warned the world about the danger of underestimating the power of the underdog.

CLARA: All the veterans and warriors, merchants and gamblers, mothers and children, the big and little people who rest here in the thousands, still living in their tombs and graves, helping us to understand, to comprehend, our own lives our history, our brilliant future. And so. Farewell for now . . .

(Voices fade out as end music "Going Home" begins under.)

> . Going Home, Going Home
> I'm a going home—
> No more tears, no more fears
> I'm a going home
>
> Down that road, No heavy load
> Never more to roam
> No more toil, no more strife
> I'll be going home
>
> Don't weep for me, I'll be free
> No more burdens bare
> 'Buked and scorned never more
> I'm a going home
> I'm a going home

(Players dance a ghostly waltz. Clara returns to her tomb as lights fade.)

THE END

Left to right: Artemisia Bowden and actor Cassandra L. Small.
Photo montage by Leland A. Qutz, from the *San Antonio Express-News*,
"In Search of a Legend" (November 13, 1998) by Kristina Paledes.

Miss Bowden's Dream

a play with music

Note: As You Read *Miss Bowden's Dream . . .*

Miss Bowden's Dream is a tribute to Artemisia Bowden who joined St. Philip's Episcopal School as a teacher in 1902. She led the school until she retired in the 1960s during which time she spearheaded its development from a sewing school for girls to a thriving institution, St. Philip's College, which became an accredited part of the Alamo Community College District in 1942. The play is postmodern in its eclectic theatricality--from back lit scrim montages with projected voice and front lit newsreel headlines to traditional stage business with a plot developed with prose, poetry, and song. The headlines on the scrim help place the action of the scenes in historical context, e.g. the projection of 1942 headlines reads "War Rages in Pacific," "First Negroes serve in U.S. Marine Corps," and "Race Riots in Michigan." Actions and thoughts are occasionally revealed through the epistolary style, that is, through letters to friends and relatives.

The play has all of the traditional American musical techniques including a large group production number in the opening and closing scenes with the opportunity for choreography. Houston mixes realism and non-realism not only by having the characters frequently burst into song but also by opening the work with two historic figures from different times. Poet Phyllis Wheatley (c.1753-1784) and abolitionist and feminist Sojourner Truth (c.1797-1883), mentors of Miss Bowden (1902-1969), discuss her hard work ethic and closeness to death. Then, they gather around her, speak to her, and guide her to the other side of life. Assembling historical figures from different times to relate to each other is a theatrical technique used by classical, modern, and contemporary authors from Aristophanes' *The Frogs* (405 BCE) to George Bernard Shaw's "Don Juan in Hell" scene in *Man and Superman* (1903) to British playwright Carly Churchill's *Top Girls* (1982). Churchill assembles fictional, historical, and contemporary characters for a ladies lunch opening scene that forecasts the themes of her feminist work. Houston's innovative use of this technique allows him to foreshadow Miss Bowden's life based on her quest for education and equal rights.

The Brechtian inspired episodic structure includes not only the sweep of history over 52 years but also plot development with numerous characters in several locations. The play is an inspirational story of a courageous and talented educator achieving against the odds of poverty, segregation, and racism.

Production Notes

Miss Bowden's Dream was first produced in 1998 by JumpStart Performance Co. in the Watson Fine Arts Auditorium of St. Philip's College as a commissioned work for the college's centennial celebration with the following cast:

Phyllis Wheatley	Gertrude E. Baker
Sojourner Truth	Ruth Statham
Artemisia Bowden	Cassandra L. Small
Bishop Johnston	Larry Metcalf
Bishop Capers (voice over)	Daniel McGlaughlin
Kate	Tammy Reed
Clark-child to mature man	Jabriel Jones
Mr. Brackenridge	Larry Metcalf
Mr. McAllister	Larry Metcalf
Mrs. Gutierrez	Richard Fuentes
José Gutierrez	J. Erick Marin
Mrs. W.W. Jackson	Maggie Crosby
Jabriel Jones (voice over)	Sterling Houston
Negro Businessman (voice over)	Steve Bailey
Texas State Senator	David Castro
Students	David Castro, Delilah Devane Rachel M. Diggs, Tammy Reed, Shawanna Marshall, Inez Stringer
Neighbors	Elma J. Knowles, Maggie Crosby, Ella Edwards

Directed by Steve Bailey

Characters

Phyllis Wheatley

Sojourner Truth

Artemisia Bowden~age 22 to 90

Bishop Johnston—Episcopal Bishop

Bishop Capers

Kate-ages 7 to 40

dark-child to mature man

Mr. Brackenridge-white businessman

Mr. McAllister-white businessman

Mrs. Gutierrez

Jose Gutierrez

Mrs. Jackson

Negro businessman

State Senator

Students—various ages, young to old neighbors

Setting

San Antonio, Texas, 1902 to present

Epilogue, 1968 to present

Prologue

(Music begins in dark. Scrim is down. Lights up at center, a graduate receives a diploma. Projections of Phyllis Wheatley and Sojourner Truth on scrim.)

(1960s—STUDENT dressed in cap and gown sings in spotlight)

> Phyllis Wheatley and
> Sojourner Truth
> were always her inspiration
> Helping her to be the very best she could be
> With words of faith and consolation;
> But there is one, I say
> Who is as great as they ...
> Artemisia Bowden, is like a mother to me
> Because of her I am proud
> To say
> I'm educated in the modern way
> Because of Miss Bowden
> My future looks very bright.
> And I, for one, am so very grateful,
> I praise her morning, noon and night ...
> Morning, noon and night.

(Chorus of STUDENTS dressed in various working attire: nurse, mechanic, chef, scholar, librarian, artist, etc. enter and join singing.)

> Phyllis Wheatley and
> Sojourner Truth
> Were always her inspiration
> Helping her to be the very best she could be
> With words of faith and consolation;
> But there is one, I say
> Who to me is as great as they ...
> Artemisia Bowden, is like a mother to me
> Because of her I am proud
> To say
> I'm educated in the modern way
> Because of Miss Bowden

My future looks very bright.
And I, for one, am so very grateful,
I praise her morning, noon and night..
Morning, noon and night.

(As song end projections fade into campus shot from 1968. Scrim rises. Lights up on Phyllis Wheatley and Sojourner Truth enter and walk DS as old Artemisia works DC at desk piled high with papers.)

PHYL: Look at her, Sojourner! Working like a Trojan till the very end.

SOJ: I almost hate to interrupt, she's studdin' so hard.

PHYL: She does look weary, though. Poor thing worked herself to the bone.

SOJ: Can she hear us, Phyllis?

PHYL: Not yet she can't, Sojourner, not till her breathing stops . . .

SOJ: It won't be long . . .

(ARTEMISIA picks up a book and opens it. She puts her hand to her forehead and lets book fall to the floor. She collapses onto desk.)

BOTH: *(Sing)* Artemisia? Artemisia Bowden . . .

PHYL: Let your spirit rise and come home . . .

SOJ: Come home to your peace!

ART: Phyllis Wheatley! Is it really you? Sojourner Truth, why do you come to me now?

BOTH: Your work down here is through, sister.

PHYL: And it has been well done . . .

(THEY gently take her by the arms and begin to lead her away.)

ART: *(Looks back over her shoulder.)* Is it really time to go? Seems like only yesterday I arrived from Georgia. How long ago was it?

SOJ: Long time, sister, long long time ago . . . *(The three of them disappear into a mist as lights change. Scrim down and video projection comes up on San Antonio in 1902.)*

ACT ONE

Scene 1

(1902-BISHOP JOHNSTON introductory song)

BISHOP JOHNSTON:
> My name is Bishop Steptoe Johnston
> I have lived a long and very full life.
> In the War-Between-The-States,
> I did not hesitate--
> I fought for the dear Confederacy
> But I was a younger man then
> And knew little of the true nature of life.
>
> I believed that God in his wisdom had made the white man
> Strong,
> Strong enough to dominate his darkest brothers,
> Strong enough to rule his sisters of every color.
> I proceeded to do my part
> I proceeded to do my part
> All the while ignoring
> The deep sadness in my heart of hearts.

(Spoken) The war has been over for thirty-seven years
And not much in the South has changed;
Former slaves are still chained!
Chained to the land that is not their own,
With heavy chains of poverty
Poverty and ignorance.
Many wander west and north
Wanting to be left alone
To build a family and a home
In this land that has promised all
The right to be happy and to stand tall,
To be free in the sight of God.
I heard the calling of the Lord
I vowed to do his will on Earth
To accept the challenge of my church,

To accept the challenge of my church
To educate the freedmen
To   cook and clean and sew and mend,
To help the black child to fit in
In white America.

To teach them how to read and write,
How to be clean and how to be polite
In this simple way I may atone
My former self, I may disown
And someday go before the golden throne
With my head held high.

(Young ARTEMISIA enters. She is a prim be-speckled young woman dressed in sober colors and a straw hat.)

ART: Good day, sir. I'm Artemisia Bowden.

BISHOP JOHNSTON: Welcome, welcome to San Antonio and to Saint Philip's. You are younger than I remembered . . .

ART: Thank you, Bishop Johnston. Although it is true, I have been on earth but rather briefly, I've tried not to waste my time.

BISHOP: Indeed and eh, Amen. As you know, the Episcopal Diocese of West Texas has committed funds to support St. Philip's since its founding in 1898, and you have my word that we will continue to help you financially for as long as need be. We may only be a sewing school for young colored girls, but then who knows what the future may bring. Along with sewing, we, of course, teach good citizenship and the three 'Rs.

ART: Reading, writing and arithmetic. Only one actually begins with an 'R', of course.

BISHOP: Of course . . .

ART: When will I get to see the school? I'm so anxious to get started and to meet the children. Just how many girls are now enrolled?

BISH. J.: Yes, of course my dear, its right next door to the church here. *(They walk. Projection of Church and Original Building in La Villita)* I bought this little piece of property for a song and built this brick school house for the princely sum of One Thousand and Eight-hundred dollars. Upstairs there's a room for you to live in.

ART: Oh, it's quite nice, Bishop. How many students did you say?

BISH: At present only twenty one. Some of our neighbors are afraid to send their children to school. But we've got to change that. We have set some modest goals. To give our students the basic skills they need to survive, but there are those who do not share our point of view, I'm afraid.

ART: Have you been threatened?

BISH: Threatened and worse . . . But I just take it to the Lord in prayer and then press on. Many of our white brethren seem determined to keep the Colored in ignorance.

ART: I'm sad to say it's the same in Georgia. Our people thought our troubles would be over with emancipation, but that was just the beginning.

BISH: Yes indeed, and this work that God has chosen us for is essential if we are to ever hold our heads up high as a nation. For knowledge is light, Miss Bowden, it's as simple as that.

BISHOP: (Sings)
> As we try to heal the nation
> There is one thing we must do.
> We must require education
> For every man and every woman too
>
> When we acquire skills and knowledge,
> We will be sure that come what may
> What we learn
> In school and college time cannot ever take away
> . . . Time cannot ever take away!

(Scene transforms during song to classroom with three or four students entering, greeting Miss Bowden, and taking a seat as she sings.)

> If we make a firm foundation
> And learn to build upon it carefully
> With faith and health and education
> We can be the way we want to be.
> When we acquire skills and knowledge,

We will be sure that come what may
That what we learn in school and College
Time cannot ever take away . . .
Time cannot ever take away

(BISH exits. ART sees a barefoot girl keeping herself shy of the others. She motions for her to join them, she shakes her head at first but after more coaxing she joins the others. MUSIC UNDER.)

ART: What's your name, child?

CHILD: Kate . . .

ART: Well, Kate? Would you like to come and join our class? We'd love to have you. Wouldn't we children?

ALL: Yes Miss Bowden . . .

KATE: I would ma'am, only . . .

ART: Well?

KATE: Only, we ain't got no money, Miss.

ART: *(She corrects)* We don't have any money.

KATE: You don't got none neither?

ART: Can you recite the alphabet, Kate?

KATE: Most of 'em! ABCDEFG-HUK-LMNOXYZ-!

ART: That's good enough for now. Help her children.

(CHILDREN join in song.)

ABCDEFG, HIJK, LMNOP-
QRSTUV, WX, Y AND Z.

One two, buckle my shoe,
Three four shut the door
Five six pick up sticks,
Seven eight, lay them straight
Nine ten, the big fat hen,
Go back to one and start again . . .

A noun is the name
Of a person place or thing

"I" before "e" except after "c"

A verb is a word
In which action has occurred . . .

Seven times nine equals sixty-three!

When we acquire skills and knowledge,
We will be sure that come what may
That what we learn in school and College
Time cannot ever take away
Time cannot ever take away!

(As song ends, a brick crashes through a window and lands at MISS BOWDEN's feet. Students huddle in fear as she retrieves the brick which has a note attached to it. She picks it up and reads.)

ART: Black Monkeys! Go back to Africa. *(She crumples note and pockets it.)* Students, we can't allow ourselves to be detracted from our lessons by people who choose to remain ignorant. Fetch a broom and we'll clean this mess and begin at the beginning. Now. Where were we? Yes. The Alphabet.

"A" is for America, the land of the free
"B" is for beyond the blue or black like you and me
"C" is for community our home sweet home
"D" is for dear duty, the source of truth and beauty
"E" is for Education for everyone!

Scene 2

(Scrim down. Projection of Edward Bowden. ARTEMISIA in her room on raised scaffold writes a letter.)

ART: *(Behind scrim)*
Dear Edward,
Things are difficult here at my little school, but full of rewarding surprises. I hope all is well with you in your medical studies. It's hard to believe that soon you will be a full fledged doctor. Our dear mother is smiling down from heaven, I know, with tears of pride. St. Philip's has

been a challenge, but I am learning every day, along with the children. We work on the same basis as a public school. We open every morning with a song of devotion, and have four sewing lessons per week, and one cooking class plus instruction on the running of an efficient household. Of course, we instruct in spelling, reading, arithmetic, geography and American history as well. Thank you for your donation of twenty dollars, I know that you make it with no small sacrifice to your own needs, and accept it in that spirit. We are much in need of everything. Especially books, paper, more and better cooking utensils and a refrigerator for the next school year.

May God's love be with you, as is my own,

Your Sister Artemisia

Scene 3

(Scrim projections to 1909 headlines etc. "Jack Johnson becomes first Negro Heavyweight Champ"--" Henson Places US Flag at North Pole" -- "Race Riot Erupts in Illinois." ART crosses down to center a U.S. projection fades in. Group of young students, now including a boy [CLARK] set "classroom" props. ART puts on teacher's smock over her dress and stands before map.)

ART: Geography is the study of the land and the countries and cities and villages on the earth. Earth as you probably know is a vast watery sphere spinning in a path around the sun. On the surface there is land and water and all of us. As for the rest of the universe, we can only guess. (US map in place) We can be sure that we and all the people we know come from places on this map. I come from right here. (Points to Georgia on map) Can you tell me what state I'm indicating?

STU: That's the state of Georgia, Miss.

ART: That's correct. And where do you come from?

STU: Columbus . . .

ART: Georgia or Ohio?

STU: No Ma'am; Texas.

ART: Let's talk about Texas . . .

CLARK: I want to be a teacher, like you Miss Bowden

ART: That's good. There's always a need for good teachers.

KATE: I wanna be a teacher, too.

CLARK: No you don't, neither!

ART: That's 'either'... double negative...

KATE: I do so.

ART: Children . . . We can be sure that we and all the people we know come from places on this map. I come from right here. *(Points to Georgia on map)* Can you tell me what state I'm indicating?

STU: That's the state of Georgia, Miss.

ART: That's correct. And where do you come from?

STU: Columbus . . .

ART: Georgia or Ohio?

STU: No Ma'am; Texas.

ART: Let's talk about Texas . . .

CLARK: I want to be a teacher, like you Miss Bowden.

ART: That's good. There's always a need for good teachers.

KATE: I wanna be a teacher, too.

CLARK: No you don't, neither!

ART: That's 'either'... double negative...

KATE: I do so.

ART: Children . . .

CLARK: Do not. Copy Cat.

KATE: Do so!

ART: You may both be teachers. However if you keep up this behavior, you might not live long enough to reach that worthy goal.

CLARK: But Miss . . .

ART: Don't make me repeat myself. Now open your books to chapter 5 . . . *(Lights fade. Projection of Edward over 'map' STUDENTS exit as ART sits at desk and writes a letter.)*

(ART. Voice Over)

ART:
Dear Edward,
The years here at St. Philip's have gone so quickly. Now that I am principal responsible for the teachers and students, have little time for contemplation or reflection, with the pressing business of St. Philip's always demanding my close attention. We are much in dept, with prices rising every day. Next semester we have to raise our tuition to one dollar, and even then must depend on the charity of generous friends. I hope, dear brother, that you are able to help with another stipend this month. I regret having to add further to your already heavy load, but with your help and the Lord's, we can get through this trial as we have all others before . . .

Scene 4

(Projections of 1919 headlines. "Du Bois Convenes First Pan-African Congress"--"Pollard becomes first Afro-American Football Player"-"Red Summer of Hate Results in Many Deaths." KATE at blackboard writing multiplication tables. ART enters.)

ART: I've been going over the bills again. It's worse than I thought. We've got to do something Kate, if we increase enrollments soon, we might be able to see our way through with the added tuitions. We could take in boarding students if we had more land . . .

KATE: All it takes is money. We could buy the house next door and put up ten more girls if we had it. Wouldn't the good Christian merchants of downtown San Antonio love that! Another bunch of little pickaninnies going back and forth frightening off their carriage trade!

ART: Kate please don't speak ill of others, especially when it's the truth.

KATE: They don't let the young ones go in the front of the general store even when we have a penny or two. Have to go around to the alley like dogs begging for bones.

ART: I wish we could re-locate. Someplace where we can grow. Our neighbors, except for a few decent souls, have never wanted colored improvement so near to them.

KATE: They think our presence brings down their property values.
ART: Bishop Johnston might be able to help. I know he will! His commitment to our cause is strong. I'll write him and state our dilemma.

KATE: At least somebody understands how much you have helped this town with your work. I'll always be grateful to you for taking me in when I was little and teaching me. I don't know what I would have done if . . .

ART: Kate dear, I don't know what I would do without your help, it's been a fair trade, I believe.

STUDENT: Miss Bowden, we have the tuition from the new students. Shall I bring it in?

ART: Please. *(STU. exits and returns with produce and caged chickens etc. CLARK enters with her. He is a young man.)* At least we have those barter students. If it wasn't for them paying tuition with chickens, cornmeal and collard greens we might all be hungry as well as poor.

MR. CLARK: *(Carrying papers)* The petition drive is going well. We've got more than five-hundred signatures, and we've just started. They can't refuse to make St. Philip's part of the school district when they see how much support we have.

ART: That's wonderful, Mr. Clark because I'm determined to take this little school to its full potential. Our future depends upon it. I dream of someday making St. Philip's into an institution of higher learning. To do that, we'll need to expand our curriculum. We'll continue to teach the principles of home-making and manual arts, but we'll need a science teacher, a music teacher . . . Step by step, year by year we can make it happen. I know it! There must be a place for our students to continue to work and to learn.

KATE: That would be nothing short of a miracle, as I'm sure you are aware. You could never be content with what you have, could you? Always pushing for more . . .

ART: You're right. But with your help, and God's grace, we can do anything. There's a little bit of property I've had my eye on for a while. Just to the east of New Braunfels Ave. A big house and two small buildings adjacent to an old dairy farm. That means good arable land with all that natural fertilizer. There's plenty of room to grow when the time comes. We can raise our tuitions and even take in boarding students. My brother Edward will help, I know he will. and the nice Miss Elenore Brackenridge and her brother. We will change the name to St. Philip's Normal and Industrial School. We'll teach teachers, plus trade skills as well as domestic ones. Why not? If we don't do it, nobody will do it for us.

I DREAM OF A WORLD (ART sings)

> Education is a key
> That opens many a door,
> But to live on earth successfully,
> We must do even more . . .
>
> I dream of a world
> Where justice falls down like rain
> Where the only thing to hate
> Is hatred and pain
>
> With Mothers and fathers enough
> To love every child
> So the children don't have to grow up
> To be lonesome and wild.
> I dream of that world I dream of that world

(KATE and CLARK join song)

> I dream of a day when sisters can walk in the sun
> With brothers beside them-
> Many hearts are stronger than one
> I dream of a world when all sleepers will waken and say
> The dream that I've dreamed of so long is living today!
> Is living today.
>
> I dream of a world
> Where justice falls down like rain-¬
> Where the only thing to hate
> Is hatred and pain.

With Mothers and fathers enough
To love every child so the Children don't have to grow up
To be lonesome and wild.

I dream of that world
I dream of that world
I dream of a day when sisters can walk in the sun
With brothers beside them--
Many hearts are better than one
I dream of a world when all dreamers will waken and say

The dream that I've dreamed of so long is living today!
Is living today.

(Scrim down. Voice Over of JOHNSTON making a speech while projections of early East Side campus and buildings are projected.)

BISHOP JOHNSTON: *(On scaffold behind scrim.)* The Colored people have been made a part of our population by a Providential dispensation which brought them here in bondage. To their unrequited labor before their emancipation, the prosperity of the Old South was largely due. I myself have been greatly indebted to them; and have tried to make some compensation to them, by fitting them for the citizenship which has been thrust upon them. During the twenty-five years of Miss Bowden's faithful work at St. Philips Industrial School, I can testify to the great improvement in every way of those who have come under her influence. There was no part of my work in which I took a deeper interest than in this school. I am an old man now. If any persons desire to erect some suitable memorial to me, when I am gone, there is nothing that would give me more pleasure than to have St. Philips selected for that purpose. I wish you the greatest success in your work, and a great reward from our Lord in His approval of something so well done. (Lights fade on scaffold as Johnston Hall- is projected.)

Scene 5

(ART at desk: GHOST PHYLLIS and SOJOURNER move about unseen by the living.)

STU: There's some one here to see you Miss Bowden, a woman and a boy.

STU: I'm not sure, I can't understand a thing she's saying except, por favor, Senorita Bowden . . .

ART: Show them in, please. *(Well dressed Mexican woman and teenage boy enter.)*

MRS. GU1TERREZ: Por favor, con su permiso, Mi hijo José, quiere entrar a su escuela, me entiende?

ART: Who are they dear?

ART: I'm afraid I only "entiende" very little . . .

JOSE: I will translate for her. I'm José. *(They shake hands)* Please to meet you.

ART: Mucho gusto.

MRS. GUTTERREZ: *(Explains the story in Spanish, as JOSE repeats it in English)*

JOSE: My son, Jose, is a very smart boy who learns fast and has good manners. I am now a citizen of this country and I like it here very much. But, I regret to say, none of the American schools will take him as a student.

ART: And why do you think that is?

JOSE: I thought that maybe it was because of his accent, but his English is very good, no?

ART: Yes.

JOSE: So one man, took me aside, he felt sorry for me I guess, and he said it was because of his color.

ART: His color?

JOSE: Yes, you see he was afraid that the other students would think he was too black to be a Mexican, and people would get the wrong idea. Do you understand?

ART: I'm afraid I do . . . I don't quite know what to say, except, Jose Gutierrez, bienvenido to St. Philip's! Tuition for one year is 18 dollars. (She pays cash as lights fade.)

Scene 6

(1929—Headlines projected "Negros Suffer Worse After Stock Market Crash"—"Nine Blacks Lynched in 1928-Lowest Number in Forty Years"—)

BISHOP CAPERS: *(Projection Photo with Voice Over)*
Dear Miss Bowden,
As we all know, St. Philip's represents the only effort on the part of the Church of the Province of the Southwest to give Negroes a practical preparation for life's work. However, owing to the failure of the people of Texas to sell their cotton, wool and cattle, except at far below market prices, your school will receive no assistance from the Diocese at the present time. For those reasons it has become necessary for you to appeal to any other source of financial aid that you can find.
With regret,
Bishop William Capers, Episcopal Bishop of West Texas.

(ART and KATE DS in office)

ART: Here's a letter from the American Church Institute for Negroes. You read it.

KATE: *(Takes letter and reads)* Dear Miss Bowden, due to your exemplary efforts accomplishments, we the American Church Institute for Negroes, will from here on provide St. Philips with an annual fund of two-thousand dollars!

ART: When one door closes, another one opens . . .

STATE SENATOR: *(Lights dim. Projection of Texas Senator.)* Educating the Negro is an infernal waste of time. It is also a gross misuse of running loose and acting superior. Next they'll be wanting to vote and run for congress . . . limited public monies. Society must ask itself it we can cope with a bunch of educated Negroes.

SOJOURNER: I want women to have their rights. In the courts women have no rights, no voice; nobody speaks for them. I wish woman to have her voice. If the courts are not a fit place for women, it is also unfit for men to be there. I suppose I am the only colored woman that goes about to speak for the rights of colored women. I want to keep the thing stirring, now that the ice is cracked. What we want is a little money. When we get our rights, we shall not have to come to you for money, for then we shall have money enough in our own pockets; and maybe you will ask us for money. But help us now until we get it. I am glad to see that colored men are getting their rights, but I want women to get theirs, and while the water is stirring I will step into the pool. I am sometimes told that "Women ain't fit to vote. What, don't you know that a woman has seven devils in her?" Seven devils ain't no account. A man has a legion in him. The man is so selfish that he has got women's rights and his own too. He keeps them all to himself.

ART: *(Flashback to slavery scene. Light up on group of slaves behind scrim picking cotton while overseer looks down from scaffold. One falls and two others help him up as overseer threatens with whip. Lights fade as projection of NEGRO LEADER fades in.)*

PHYLLIS W: I, young in life, by seeming cruel fate
Was snatch'ed from Africa's fancy'd happy seat:
What pangs excruciating must molest,
What sorrows labour in my parent's breast?
Steel'd was the soul and by no misery moved
That from a father seiz'd his babe beloved
Such, such my case. And can I then but pray
Others may never feel tyrannic sway.

NEGRO BUSINESSMAN: *(Projection with Voice Over)* St. Philip's must close down. Not because Miss Bowden has not made the maximum effort, but because it is far inferior to the white school, San Antonio College. It should be closed, and let taxpayers of color demand admission to San Antonio College, since their taxes go to support a system which has excluded them by law and custom. This is clearly Taxation without Representation and it must be changed. Let St. Philip's close so that its students may get a proper education for the years ahead . . . !

(Lights up on scaffold as family group reacts in shock at sight of lynched man. They take him down and weep. Lights down.)

ART: *(In front of scrim)* Well, Lord, you've brought us from a mighty long way. For that I'm truly thankful. But it seems our struggles are never ending . . . and it just doesn't gets any easier, does it? . . .

(Lights fade as music swells I DREAM theme. End of Act One)

ACT TWO

Scene 1

(1930—Headlines: "Billy Holiday begins Singing Career"--"Delta Sigma Theta Sorority Incorporated"--"Scottsboro Boys Trial begins Before All White Jury")

(CLARK returns from the Army still wearing his sergeant's uniform. He tip-toes behind KATE who sits reading, and blindfolds her with his hands)

CLARK: Guess who?

KATE: Clark! I can't believe it's really you.

CLARK: You're all grown up.

KATE: You are too. What happened?

CLARK: Don't know. Just a miracle of time, I guess. How're your Mama and Dad?

KATE: Everyone's doing fine. It's so nice to see you.

CLARK: Good to see, you too, Kate.   Thanks for writing to me overseas. A letter from home to a soldier is the next best thing to a home cooked meal.

KATE: I missed you so much. I mean . . .

CLARK: I know what you mean.

KATE: Was it just awful, being stationed over there?

CLARK: It was my duty. That's the main thing, isn't it? Now that we've marched and worked shoulder-to-shoulder, white and black together, we'll get the respect we've always deserved. How's Miss Bowden?

KATE: Same as ever. Working too hard and keeping us all together.

CLARK: I want to apply here at St. Philip's for a teaching position. Do you think she'd have me?

KATE: You know she would. What do you want to teach?

CLARK: Electronics. You know, radio. You must have heard about it even in sleepy old San Antonio.

KATE: Well, of course.

CLARK: It's wide open for people trained in electronic technology. And I could train them. I learned all about it in the service. How to make radios, fix them, invent new ones. The sky's the limit, and we could be on the ground floor. The Colored man could earn a decent living in a field with a future!

KATE: Clark, that's wonderful . . . only . . .

CLARK: Only what . . .

KATE: Money. Or the lack of it. We don't get paid much, nor very often. But we have food and shelter, and more students every year, thanks to Miss Bowden's determination.

CLARK: And you?

KATE: Me?

CLARK: Pretty woman, like you. Don't you have a steady beaux?

KATE: Are you courting me, Mr. Clark?

CLARK: Believe I am, Miss Kate.

KATE: That's . . . nice.

CLARK: Goshamighty, girl. I've been plum crazy about you ever since you asked me to that Sadie Hawkins Dance in 1919.

KATE: Yes. And you kept trying to sneak a peek at my ankles . . .

CLARK: Some things never change . . .

(Flashback-SADIE HAWKINS DANCE. Banners, paper decorations, balloons, etc. drop in. Chorus of STUDENTS enter. Mis-matched couples dance. SONG sung by female STUDENT)

"IF EVERY DAY WAS SADIE HAWKINS DAY"

If every day was Sadie Hawkins Day
Then hens would crow

And the roosters start to lay
Bachelors would be a thing of the past

When brides propose, and Grooms say yes
If I had my way on Sadie Hawkins Day
Miss Sadie she can do the Bunny Hop
But don't you let her do the Eagle Rock
Girls are shy and boys are bold

But Sadie Hawkins ain't been told
Turn about is fair play
On Sadie Hawkins Day!

(DANCE sequence)

If every day was Sadie Hawkins Day
Then Hens would crow
And the roosters start to lay
Bachelors would be a thing of the past
When brides propose, and Grooms say yes
If I had my way on Sadie Hawkins Day
Miss Sadie she can do the Bunny Hop
But don't you let her do the Eagle Rock
Girls are shy and boys are bold
But Sadie Hawkins ain't been told
Turn about is fair play
On Sadie Hawkins Day!

(ART enters scene. At first she is prim and then begins to pat her foot to rhythm. She picks one of the boys to dance with her. They do a show-stopping cake-walk-style dance as others cheer them on.)

If every day was Sadie Hawkins Day
Then Hens would crow
And the roosters start to lay
Bachelors would be a thing of the past
When brides propose, and Grooms say yes
If I had my way on Sadie Hawkins Day
Miss Sadie she can do the Bunny Hop
But don't you let her do the Eagle Rock
Girls are shy and boys are bold
But Sadie Hawkins ain't been told

Turn about is fair play
On Sadie Hawkins Day!

Scene 2

(Scrim down. Headlines 1935 "Pres. Roosevelt Takes Action to End Depression."—"First Negro Democratic Congressman Elected"— "Mary McLeod Bethune Founds the National Council of Negro Women" projected. ART sits in office reading. Loud crash off stage.)

ART: What in the . . .

STU.: Miss Bowden! Miss Bowden! the roof just caved in the science room! Miss Bowden—there's no flour to make bread for supper! Again.

ART: I'll better go see George Brackenridge. He's a good man of business; he and his sister have been major contributors to St. Philip's. Surely he doesn't want to see his investment go bad! Bills must be paid. Even during this depression. *(Puts on hat and coat and 'travels' to Mr. Bracken ridge's office which is projected on screen.)*

(Sings)
Oh Mr. Brackenridge, Oh Mr. Brackenridge, this is your old friend Artemisia Bowden—

(BRACK. appears in light on scaffold behind scrim.)

MR. B: Hello, Artemisia! How are things at school?

ART: Well since you asked sir, they could be better—My teachers haven't been paid In more than seven months, sir. Could you help us out with a small donation? Oh, it would mean so much, We do need books and such and oil to warm us in the coming winter. ¬Could you see you way to, say, one-hundred dollars?

MR. B.: Why don't we say Fifteen Dollars!

ART:
I thank you, yes indeed
I thank you, yes indeed
For helping my people in a time of great need.

MR. B.: Alright, twenty-five dollars, and that's all I can afford.

ART: Thank you from the bottom of my heart.

STU: *(Off-stage sounds of hissing water and commotion)* Miss Bowden! Miss Bowden, the plumbing's all backed up in the boys lavatory and it smells something awful! Miss Bowden, we're out of paper again!

ART: What kind of paper?

STU: All kinds . . .

ART: I better get busy . . . Young Walter McAllister is always ready to help. I'll go visit him at his real-estate office.

(ART crosses to another office, projection of 30s store front fades into face of young Walter.)

Mr. McAllister, Mr. McAllister. This is your old friend, Artemisia Bowden.

MR. M.: Hello, Artemisia. How are things at school?

ART: Well, since you asked sir, they could be better. The roof leaks so bad we wear raincoats in the classroom. Our books are out of date. We're out of chalk and slate. We can no longer wait to pay the plummer— Could you see your way today to give us a small donation?

MR. M: Alright Artemesia,

ART: Thank you, bless you, Mr. McAllister

MR. M: *(Sighs as he writes check)* Promise me you'll do something about the permanent financial crisis at St Philip's.

ART: Believe me, believe me; nothing would please me more *(MR. M. fades out. Lights change.)*

STUDENT: Here it is Miss Bowden. Hot off the press *(Hands her a copy of The Tiger)*

ART: I'm so proud of you students. Look at this! Our very own campus newspaper! We've made such strides between the hardships we've had to endure. We've just got to find a way to get more property. With the corner lot and the double lot across the way, we could take in more boarding students which would raise our income by a considerable sum. *(Art puts on her hat and coat and grabs a large tin cup.)*

STU: Where are you going?

ART: I'm tired of waiting for money from the mail. I'm going out fundraising! *(Sings)*
>Hello dear neighbor, Hello dear neighbor
>It's just your old friend Artemisia Bowden

NEIGHBOR: Afternoon, Miss Bowden. How are things with you?

ART: *(Sings)*
>I'm going door to door
>To ask the neighbors for
>Whatever they can spare, to keep us going . . .

STUDENTS: *(Sing)*
>She's going door to door
>To ask the neighbors for
>Whatever they can spare, to keep us going . . .

ART:
>You know how much we've done
>With very little funds,
>With your kind help today
>We can keep growing . . .

NEIGH.: *(Sings)*
>I'll try to do my part.   Not much
>But it's a start
>I'll try to do my part
>To keep things going . . .
>Thank you dear neighbor. Thank you dear neighbor
>From the bottom of my heart.

ART: *(Sings)*
>Hello dear neighbor. Hello dear neighbor.
>It's just your old friend Artemisia Bowden.

NEIGHBOR: Afternoon, Miss Bowden. How are things with you?

ART: *(Sings)*
>I'm going door to door
>To ask the neighbors for
>Whatever they can spare, to keep us going . . .

STUDENTS: *(Sing)*
>She's going door to door
>To ask the neighbors for
>Whatever they can spare, to keep us going . . .

ART: *(Sings)*
>You know how much we've done
>With very little funds,
>With your kind help today
>We can keep growing . . .

NEIGH.: *(Sings)*
>I'll try to do my part.   Not much
>But it's a start
>I'll try to do my part
>To keep things going . . .

ART: *(Sings)*
>Thank you dear neighbor,
>Thank you dear neighbor
>From the bottom of my heart.

KATE: Miss Bowden, this just came special delivery . . . *(She gives letter to Art.)*

ART: This to certify that St. Philips Industrial School having fully met the requirements of the State of Texas can now be designated as a Class "A" Junior College. At last! We did it! I knew we could!

(Reprise.)

Scene 3

(Projection of 1939 Headlines: "Hitler invades Poland"—"Hattie McDaniel First Negro to win Academy Award"—"DAR Bars Marian Anderson from Singing at Constitution Hall")

(ART in office speaks on phone to KATE)

ART: I'm wanted as a guest speaker at the national meeting of Outstanding Negro Women of America. It means going to Washington D.C. for a week or so. They will pay me $50 dollars and of course, I will plead our case to them for a large donation!

KATE: When one door closes, another one opens . . .

ART: You and Mr. Clark must take care of everything while I'm away. It may be as longer than   a week.

KATE: Don't worry. We'll manage fine. *(sotto voice)* I hope and pray.

ART: I think it's so sweet that you and Mr. Clark are courting.

KATE: Is it that obvious?

ART: I've known you both since you were children. Not much gets by me.

KATE: Miss Bowden. Don't you ever miss it? You know, getting married and having a family of your own?

ART: Kate dear, you and every student who's passed through this school, you are all my children. I have a great big family!

KATE: Have a wonderful trip, and don't worry we'll take care of everything . . .

(Lights fade)

Scene 4

(Video of 1930s passenger train in motion. Projection fades as Art speaks from scaffold.)

ART: Democracy bases its hopes for continuity upon education of its masses, however, educational opportunities are not equal for all citizens. Negroes are not being given equal educational opportunities. Inequalities in educational opportunities make for inequalities in citizenship status. A growing sense of the injustices of this situation is gradually taking form as people realize that an active concern for the welfare of all, is essential to the success of a Democratic nation. That as long as we have discontentment and ignorance which enslaves, there will be less freedom and less security for all. The American character, whatever its shortcomings, abounds in courage, creative energy and resourcefulness, and is founded upon the profound conviction that nothing in the world is beyond its power to accomplish. Every soul has an inherent right to all possible aid to perfect his character. We must have a democracy that in essential needs, makes no differentiation between rich and poor nor black and white.

(Lights fade with applause)

Scene 5

(Lights up DS. Some days later in office. It is dusk and lights dim slowly throughout scene.)

CLARK: Now, remember, when Miss Bowden gets here let me do the talking. We don't want her to get upset.

KATE: How could they do it, Mr. Clark? Leave us in the cold and dark! Don't they know we've got to have classes?

CLARK: It's strictly business, nothing personal against us. We'll just have to raise the money to pay the bills, that's all.

STUDENT: Here they come . . . *(ART and 2nd STUDENT enter with suitcases from trip)*

CLARK: Welcome back, Miss Bowden . . . Did you have a nice trip?

ART: Thank you, it was fine, not as lucrative as I had hoped . . .

KATE: That's nice . . .

CLARK: Real nice.

ART: Why is everyone so glum?

KATE: We've got a little problem with the electricity, you see . . .

ART: They shut us off?

KATE: Yes Ma'am, now we're in the cold and dark. *(She weeps)* We've got classes to conduct on Monday! What'll we do?

ART: Mr. Clark, you remember the times before we had electricity. What did we do then?

CLARK: Well, we lit candles and kerosene lamps!

ART: And so we shall now! Kate, find me some matches if you please.

KATE: But it's 1939! We've gotten used to these modern conveniences . . .

ART: It will only be a temporary return to our earlier days.

KATE: What are you made of? Doesn't anything get you down?

CLARK: Kate . . .

ART: Don't worry, Kate. We'll straighten out the bill and be back to normal directly. Just be thankful that the Lord has seen fit that we have a supply of candles and matches to light them!

(During song, ART lights one candle, and from her light one by one all candles are lit until entire ensemble is illuminated.)

(Sings)
>   We struggle here alone and wonder
>   why burdens seem so hard to overcome.
>   We try to keep our people warm and dry
>   while teaching mathematics and the fall of Rome.
>
>   Then I remember my dear mother's words.
>   Sweeter than the sound of summer rain.
>   I take heart and try to carry on.
>   Knowing that the clouds will clear again . . .
>
>   With grace from God
>   I can do anything . . .
>   I can do anything
>   With grace from God
>
>   When times get hard
>   And seem impossible
>   Nothing's impossible
>   With grace from God

(Others join in song)
>   With grace from God
>   We can do anything . . .
>   We can do anything
>   With grace from God

When times get hard
And seem impossible
Nothing's impossible
With grace from God

With grace from God
We can do anything . . .
We can do anything
With grace from God

*(During song, projections of lighted candles double-exposed over images of
St. Philip's buildings evolving from the 20s to the 40s Buildings fade out
and leave projection of field of lit white candles echoed by the 'live' candles
held by company on stage.)*

Scene 6

*(1942—Projection of 1942 Headlines. "War Rages in Pacific" —"First
Negroes serve in U.S. Marine Corps"—"Race Riots Rock Michigan." Fade
to photo of Mrs. W.W. Jackson, White matron, voice over speaks)*

JACKSON: Through these many years my personal friendship has
continued to grow as my appreciation increases year by year for my
good friend Artemisia Bowden, who is today being honored . . . I consider it a privilege to be asked to add a few words to the praise lavishly
given by others to this distinguished citizen of San Antonio and the
State of Texas. But the honors received go beyond mere state bound-
aries. On the national level, Miss Bowden was given an award as one
of the twelve outstanding women in the United States. This award is
made annually and others who have received the same citation include
Mrs. Mary McCloud Bethune and Mrs. Eleanor Roosevelt. All of this
is added to her outstanding achievement in education at St. Philip's
College. She has opened doors of understanding for all regardless of
race, creed or color, and has sponsored true dignity in others.

Mrs W.W. Jackson,
Executive Office
Southern Methodist University

Scene 7

(DS Graduation 1942. Students in cap and gown as EDUCATION theme plays. MISS BOWDEN has aged. Student speaks from podium.)

VALEDICTORY STUDENT: . . . And so, with great pleasure, I introduce our spiritual founder and leader, Miss Artemisia Bowden . . . *(Applause as ART rises and goes to podium.)*

ART: Ever since St. Philip's was a one-room school in old downtown San Antonio, this day has been my dream . . . a dream which has sustained me through good and bad times. Now as I see your beautiful faces, filled with hope and pride, I know that the dream was little compared with the reality of today. In this year, St. Philip's Junior College has become an institution of higher learning within the San Antonio Independent School District, and will be funded by the tax dollars of the city and county. We are now San Antonio College, St. Philip's Branch. (Applause) My message to you graduates is a simple one. Walk tall, for you have so much to live for. You are the ones who must see that all men and all women rise to fulfill their maximum potential. You are the ones who must see to it that the great creative spirit within us all be allowed to shine at its very brightest magnitude, freed from the shackles of fear, poverty and ignorance. For my generation has done what we could, but now, the task falls to you. You are the best we have.

(Song reprise)

(Collage of projections of St. Philip's buildings and faces of students and teachers through the decades. Graduate chorus and Ensemble sing)

(Reprise)

> Phyllis Wheatley and
> Sojourner Truth
> Were always her inspiration
> Helping her to be the very best me
> With words of faith and inspiration;
> But there is one, I say
> Who to me is as great as they . . .

(During following, Ghost Phyllis and Sojourner enter and take ART. to "Heaven" on scaffold behind scrim. Waiting for her there are Bishop Johnston, Frederick Douglass, Booker T. Washington, Harriet Tubman, and other Black Pantheon figures. They make a place for ART, and she receives her wings.)

Artemisia Bowden, is like a mother to me
Because of her I am proud
To say
I'm educated in the modern way
Because of Miss Bowden
My future looks very bright.
And I, for one, am so very grateful,
I praise her morning, noon and night . . .
Morning, noon and night.

(Music changes to fat beat, lights down on ART and pantheon. Graduate Chorus breaks into dance formation. Students sing.)

If you take a'hold of my hand
(My hand!)
I will take you to the promised land!
If you hear the beat of my feet
(My feet!)
Get up and dance around your seat—
We know who we are (We are)
We're not turning back we've come too far.
We know who we are (We are)
We're not turning back we've come too far.
And we got something to sing about—
It took a hundred years to work it on out,
We got something to shout out loud—
From deep inside and it must come out—
We got something to tell the world—
Every man and woman, boy and girl-
We got something to celebrate
A hundred years old and doing great!
If you take a'hold of my hand
(My hand!)
I will take you to the promised land!
If you hear the beat of my feet

(My feet!)
Get up and dance around your seat—
We know who we are
(We are)
We're not turning back

We've come too far.
We know who we are
(We are)
We're not turning back
We've come too far.
We have made the big turnaround
black, and white and yellow and brown!

Together we can do this difficult thing!
With a little bit of money and a lot of brains.
We got something to tell the world—
every man and woman, boy and girl—
We got something to celebrate
A hundred years old and doing great!
We dream of a world when the dreamers
will waken and say
That old dream that I dreamed of so long
is living today!

(Projections conclude with faces of current students, cast members, faculty, and newest buildings/other campuses. Over last images the face of the real Artemisia Bowden is projected as lights fade to out. Music out)

THE END

Cameoland

A memory play with music

Note: As You Read *Cameoland*

With *Cameoland*, Sterling Houston, the historian, comes to the fore. He starts in the present and leads his audience back to the San Antonio of the 1940s and 1950s. The thirteen-scene one-act musical play is framed by a prologue and an epilogue. The focal point of the drama is the Cameo Theatre, built on the Eastside of San Antonio on Commerce Street in the 1940s. As one of the cultural centers of the community it featured musical acts, vaudeville, and movies. The play's prologue in the present (1990s), sets the scene as Bill, a graduate student working on a Ph.D. enters the Cameo Theatre hoping to interview someone who knows the history. Bill's inquiry stirs the ghosts of the Cameo, and he is thrust into the milieu of trains, '40s movies, shoeshine stands, beauty shops, and vaudeville shows. The past and present are juxtaposed as Bill, from the present, looks on and even comments on and participates in the scenes from the past.

Houston mixes video clips, narration, dialogue, and song in a nonlinear structure that highlights significant memories of his characters. Its narrative structure is in the tradition of Thornton Wilder's *Our Town*, as is its abstract depiction of place/location.

The central motif of the work is the quest—the search for something, perhaps satisfaction and significant meaning. It is first expressed as part of the action of the play in a clip from *The Thief of Bagdad*, a popular movie in the 1940s. This motif is repeated several times, with slight variations, by different characters, as below from the projected excerpt of the movie:

> He: Why have you come?
> She: To find you.
> He: Where have you come from?
> She: From the other side of time.
> He: How long have you been searching?
> She: Since time began.

The drama foregrounds dispossession in many forms—lost opportunities, love, and even home, but not without reverent nostalgia, humor, and hope.

Production Notes

Cameoland was first produced in 2003 by JumpStart Performance Co. at the Carver Community Center's Little Carver Theatre in San Antonio with the following cast:

Joe	SkudRJones
Bill	Lafollette Marquis
Helen/Montgomery Sister	Danielle Barnes
Flo/Savannah Savoy	Regina Sanders
Rose/Montgomery Sister	Alisa Claridy
Franklin/Jocko	Luther Maddox
Buddy /Jimmy	Kevin Evans
La Movida/Brown Skin Model	Deidre Lacour
Straight 8/Brown Skin Model	Andrea Wilson

Composer: Sterling Houston
Musical Arranger and Director/Composer : Tito Villalobos Moreno
Director: Steve Bailey

Characters:

Bill — Young grad student

Helen — Afro-American Matron

Flo/Savannah — A high maintenance beauty

Rose/Montgomery Sister — A flighty single woman

Franklin/Jocko — Middle age Afro-American

Buddy /Jimmy — Thirtyish Afro-American man

La Movida/Brown Skin Model

Straight 8/Brown Skin Model

Setting:

Present, flashback to 1940s and 50s, overlapping of past and present, San Antonio, Texas.

Prologue

(VIDEO of GENIE coming out of bottle. Then, lights up.)

(Ghost people: Flo, Buddy, Rose, Helen, Joe, Franklin, Dancers; the scene is sung by characters, except the section identified as whispered at the end.)

BILL: Women with lips like black cherries

JOE: Lips like black plums. Lips like wet garnets

BUDDY: Like the dark red hearts of pomegranates

FRANKLIN: Sipping on a highball

HELEN: Puffing on a Pall Mall

FLO: Lanky Women

ROSE: Luxurious Women

JOE: Cameo Women

BUDDY: Commerce Street Women

BILL: Hips in motion like an invitation to dance

FRANKLIN: Hips for holding

JOE: Hips and lips to let go most unwillingly

HELEN: Well dressed and self-possessed. Cameo Women.
　　Folks don't know
　　They just don't know
　　How far we had come from
　　How far we have to go

FLO: Men of the color of wet cinnamon
　　Lean against late Victorian doorways

HELEN: Lean on parked Buick Specials,
　　Chesterfields in Nylon pockets

ROSE: Shiny processed hair rolling like black waves
　　Shiny processed hair rolling like black waves

FLO: Lips O lips, like fresh strawberries

HELEN: Cool as a cucumber

ROSE: Hot as the Sunset—
    The Sunset Limited

HELEN: Confident men?

FLO: Confident men?

ROSE: Poised on the verge of satisfaction

JOE: Eyes deep and wide enough to contain

MEN: Oceans of pain

WOMEN: Rivers of rain

ALL: Folks don't know
    They just don't know
    How far we had to come from
    How far we have to go

ROSE: I came from New Orleans
    I'm back in San Antone
    But I'm going to Chicago
    Just as sure as you're born

    Folks don't know
    They just don't know
    How far we had to come from
    How far we have to go

JOE & FRANKLIN: I came from Alabam
    Outside of Birmingham
    But I'm going to San Antonio
    Just as fast as I can.

(All whisper)

    Without a drum
    The dreams won't come
    I might be crazy but
    I sho' ain't dumb . . .

Without a drum
The dreams won't come
I might be crazy but
I sho' ain't dumb . . .

(Sings or chants)

Folks don't know
They just don't know

Scene 1

BILL: *(A young grad student enters and makes notes on a pad. After a while, he checks his watch and calls out. Hello? (His voice echoes.) Anybody here? (to himself) (An older Black man appears out of the dark.)* Oh! Hello. Are you Mister . . .

JOE: I can help you.

BILL: Hi. I'm Bill Winters; I called about the project I'm doing.

JOE: Yeah.

BILL: The research project for my urban studies dissertation . . . about the history of this neighborhood.

JOE: That so?

BILL: Like to get stories of folks 'round here before it all changes; Civil Rights Act passed, you know. No more segregated ghettos for our people.

JOE: That's what they say. I guess.

BILL: Is it alright if I tape our interview? Just to make sure I get it right.

JOE: Have to get it right.

BILL: Do you own the Cameo?

JOE: Naw, not exactly—. I used to come here though, when I was a kid. Long, long time ago, and gone. I just watch it now, mostly.

BILL: What was this place anyway? A dancehall?

JOE: It was the Cameo Theater.

BILL: For real. So . . . they showed movies and cartoons and things?

JOE: That's right.

BILL: Vaudeville?

JOE: Uh huh. Chitlin' Circuit.

BILL: They served food too?

JOE: T.O.B.A.

BILL: Stands for Theater Owners Booking Association, or Tough on black actors.

JOE: I want to tell you something about memory.

BILL: Memory or memories?

JOE: Memory is a funny thing—kind' a slips-slides . . . This place has a lot of memories, shadows, ghosts, you know. Shadows and lights and echoes of picture shows, live shows, memories, echoes.

(Images on screen)

BILL: I don't believe in ghosts . . .

JOE: Me either. But I do believe that the dead walk around in the bodies of the living. Who really owns the past? Me or you? Who's memories are they?

BILL: I don't remember. Not mine. But I don't . . . oh yeah.

JOE: Something's happening.

Scene 2

(All singing)

> Folks don't know
> They just don't know
> How far we had come from
> How far we have to go

(Lights up on CAMEO marquee)

JOE: *(to audience)* It's a mid-summer Saturday mid-afternoon—and the sidewalk in front of the Cameo Theater is jumping with the ebb and flow of Negro life.

ROSE: The Cameo is situated on an old horse and buggy trail in San Antonio, Texas known as East Commerce Street. There was a time when Commerce was a fine place to be.

HELEN: San Antonio is like a little paradise to me.

FRANKLIN: Many fine upstanding folks! Civic leaders, doctors, teachers, lawyers, preachers – they all have a story.

JOE: Yeah, but this ain't it.

ALL: This is mine.

FLO: Cross the street over there is the Southern Pacific Station--the "S.P."for short, every day trains be rolling in from Chicago, California and points west; and other trains roll out to points south and east. Then they turn around and do it all again in reverse direction.

(Lights up on box office. ROSE puts on lipstick looking into a compact.)

JOE: That's Miss Rose. She takes the tickets at the Cameo box office and has been known as a heartbreaker. You looking extra fine today, Miss Rose . . .

ROSE: Why you telling all that stuff. Don't nobody care but you, Jojo.

JOE: Well, they need to care, that's what I'm talking about. *(Back to audience)*

FLO: On the corner of Chestnut and Commerce stood Sam Wo's, *(Lights up)* a restaurant with two front doors; one for colored and one for white.

JOE: Only had one cook and one kitchen.

ROSE: And that food is good, too. I'm talking about slap you' mamma time.

JOE: Got a long horseshoe shaped counter, serving food from the middle, to white folks on one side and Negroes on the other.

BILL: How does Mr. Sam Woo feel about that, I wonder?

JOE: Busts em' up. Old Mister Sam and his Chinese kin folks, they been a part of this neighborhood since Mister Sam's granddaddy got hisself run out of old Mexico by Poncho Villa and his boys. Bet you didn't know that 'chingao' was a Chinese word.

BILL: There was a Chinese presence in the neighborhood since the turn of the century?

HELEN: Might near. Whole family speaks mostly Spanish with a thick Cantonese accent. Next door to the Cameo is Burley's Barber Shop. You can sit there, if you want to, and listen to the ball game on the radio, find out who died, who got married, who split up, who left town and who came in, got a shave and a haircut and the best spit-shine in San Antonio.

FRANKLIN: A shine on his shoes really meant something to a fella back then, yessiree. It signified that he was a serious man and intended to make an impression on the world.

HELEN: Folks be sharp as a tack, too. Men and women.

JOE: Next to the barbershop was the House of Blue Lights. *(Lights up on juke box, music up low)* I couldn't go in the House of Blue Lights . . .

FLO: Yeah, but I could . . .

JOE: But that didn't stop me from listening to the juke-box pump out the blues onto the sidewalk.

FLO: Had the best juke-box on Commerce Street.

(Music up, "I want to know . . .") (Sound of approaching train)

ROSE: Here comes that Sunset Limited! Right on time, too.

JOE: Yeah! The first sound I ever heard was the sound of that train. But was it coming or going? That old Sunset Limited brought passengers, freight and the latest out-of-town news in stacks of newspapers—The Los Angeles Sentinel, the Pittsburg Courier, the

Amsterdam News, that would let us Texas colored folks know what was what in those big, black far away cities of America.

(Slides/Video of the period)

HELEN: And those porters, Lord have mercy, they were like angels on wheels of steel—I could have married one once, you know.

ROSE: Folks say don't ever marry no road-running man.

HELEN: Pullman porters came like a small army of uniformed cultural couriers, urban ambassadors bringing in the latest records, magazines, and hot chit-chat from every black belt boomtown where the train had a station.

ROSE: Pullman porters got paid good money too.

FRANKLIN: One of the best paying jobs a colored man could get, thanks to the efforts of Mr. A. Phillip Randolph and the Brotherhood of Sleeping Car Porters.

ROSE: I know y'all know who Mr. A. Philip Randolph is—if you don't, go read a book.

JOE: When a porter got paid he came in to San Antonio to spend his green. Lot of them, after running the road for a week or more, would come on over to Commerce Street to raise a little cane.

HELEN: Some of them might stay over at the Dunbar or the Manhattan or the Deluxe Hotel while they was in town.

JOE: Go eat over at Sam Woo's or Carpenter's Café on Cherry Street for the best enchiladas, collard greens and smothered pork chops this side of the Mississippi.

ROSE: And naturally they sought out some local diversion after dark—at night from twilight and sometimes till dawn, it was the Avalon, the Chocolate Bar . . .

HELEN: The Keyhole, the Brown Skin Grill . . .

FLO: The Froggy Bottom, the Lifesaver . . .

JOE: During the day, fella might get a haircut and a shine, or take in a picture show at the Cameo Theater. *(Lights change)*

(Singing)

> Folks don't know
> They just don't know
> How far we had come from
> How far we have to go

Scene 3

(BUDDY enters, crosses to box office area.)

ROSE: Can I help you, mister man?

BUDDY: Yes Ma'am, I'll take one ticket for the matinee, if you please.

ROSE: That'll cost you thirty-five cents, and one sweet kiss.

BUDDY: That's a bargain, baby. *(She presents her cheek, then catches him on the lips.)*

ROSE: Good to see you, Buddy. *(Caresses his cheek)* Ya miss me much?

BUDDY: Like the bee misses honey.

ROSE: Ooh, talk sweet to me baby . . .

BUDDY: I'm gone go watch the picture and let you cool down, girl.

ROSE: Cost you thirty-five cents, please. It's a double feature, baby. The kiss was free. (Buddy pays) My shift be over at eight.

BUDDY: And I won't be late. Oh, I almost forgot. Brought you a little something, too. (He hands her a magazine.)

ROSE: Oh, my Lord in the morning! A catalogue from the May Co. in Los Angeles, California! Ooooh! Thank you Buddy! Check out those hats they're wearing now. Look like you could eat one for dessert.

BUDDY: Pick yourself out something real nice, and I'll bring it to you next time, if you be a good girl.

ROSE: Don't you know I'm always good to a good man.

BUDDY: That's my woman talking, now. *(Exits into the movie as lights cross fade)*

Scene 4

(From offstage as JOE and BILL listen)

HELEN: *(As mother's voice)* Joe! Joseph! Come on in here Joe, 'fore Straight-Eight gonna get you!

BILL: Straight-Eight?

JOE: Now that's a story . . . *(continues sotto voce)*

(Video up from "The Thief of Baghdad" trailer. Then, lights up on domino game.)

Scene 5

(JOE and BILL continue interview outside on the street.)

BILL: So what you're saying is . . .

JOE: This was a real cosmopolitan boulevard; hotels, fine restaurants, entertaining diversions for the mind, body, and soul. This wasn't no little one-horse town, no indeed. Harlem didn't have a thing on Commerce Street back in those days. Still it as a real neighborhood, where everybody knew everybody. You know what? I found out something in my travels.

BILL: What's that?

JOE: Those teachers in those old segregated schools, Wheatley, and Douglass, and Booker T? They really gave me an education. When I finished high school, I knew something about the world. And about who I was.

BILL: Do you think that's going to be lost?

JOE: It's lost already. Already gone.

BILL: Strange how you don't notice things, until they're not there. Then you notice their absence.

JOE: You don't miss the water . . .

BILL: Yeah, like the song says . . .

JOE: . . .Till you well runs dry.

BILL: I almost feel it. I want to know how it really was. What it felt like.

JOE: Today is the tomorrow we were so worried about yesterday.

BILL: I don't understand.

JOE: There is a way, a place I should show you. A place in time.

BILL: Time?

JOE: Just follow my lead. Are you ready?

BILL: Let's go.

(Franklin and Buddy sit at table with a game of dominoes.)

FRANKLIN: Slap 'em down fellas. Spread 'em around, then read 'em and weep!

JOE: Come on man, let's play some dominos.

BUDDY: Don't be rushing folks. Where you been anyway? Who's your little partner?

JOE: Fellas, this is my little cousin from Houston. I'm babysitting for a while. Thought he could sit in on a game or two. Learn some stuff.

BUDDY: Big city boy form Third Ward. Can he play? You know the boy can't play no dominos.

BILL: *(Adopting a youthful naïve demeanor and language to play along with Joe)* Yes, I can too. Cain't I play more better now? Cain't I, uncle Joe? He showed me. I'm much more better, huh?

FRANKLIN: don't say 'more better' son, it's redundant. The boy's got to learn the game some kinda way. Who gone teach him if we don't?

JOE: Alright, then. Let's get with it and play, then. That's all I want to do, anyway.

BUDDY: That ain't ALL you want to do, in the least, from what I done heard . . .

FRANKLIN: Don't be hoo-rawin' that man, now just play . . .

JOE: What you mean by that, Mr. Pullman Porter man?

BILL: Don't be messing with him, Buddy. Joe'll cut you quicker than Straight-Eight.

FRANKLIN: What you know about Straight-Eight boy? Not a damn thing . . .

BILL: Yeah, I do too.

BUDDY: I knew the real Straight-Eight, and she wasn't some scary joke, neither. Just a good woman living in a bad time.

JOE: Slap it down now. Alright.

FRANKLIN: Straight-Eight ain't nobody for no young person to be emulating when they set out in life, now. The way she walked was thorny . . .

JOE: . . . Through no fault of her own.

FRANKLIN: Ended up dying in the state pen for all her cunning and native bravado.

BUDDY: Just tell me, Mr. Franklin, who you think folks be talking about in fifty years, you or Straight-Eight?

FRANKLIN: Listen here, young fella. Listen and you might learn something. Things remembered at the present time are never really recalled exactly as they were. Times of pain and terror become diminished, less vivid, like keloid scar tissue growing over what was once a bloody wound. Sweet days! Nights of black silk breezes transform when remembered into shuddering bliss. The prose of actual experience becomes the poetry of experience recalled.

BILL: Wow. He always talk like that?

JOE: He cain't help it. That's Mr. Franklin. He's a self-educated man.

FRANKLIN: So, when I tell you that in my tender boyhood, a

colored fellow couldn't walk on the sidewalk, I want you to understand that the agony that put upon my heart is all but inexpressible in the mere recitation of ordinary facts.

BUDDY: Yes sir. I hear what you're saying.

FRANKLIN: When telephones came out, Negroes couldn't get no telephones. Couldn't even get one by law. Did not want the colored to communicate over long distances—even across town; wanted to keep him picking cotton on a technological plantation.

JOJO: Sho 'nuff, you say.

FRANKLIN: Given the weight of the shackles bound around my ambition, I had but two choices: die, or become, in the eyes of my oppressor, an entrepreneurial outlaw. Folks like to say that I run the policy. I don't run the policy. The people who play the policy, which is every one who's best hope for fortune is a throw of the numbers; they run the policy. I only organize it for 'em, and keep the money in order. Everybody wins sometime. Most a little bit. Some a lot. I take a percentage and put the rest back into the community. For this the sheriff of Bexar County wants to put my entrepreneurial black ass in jail.

JOJO: You ain't no outlaw, Mr. Franklin. You a businessman!

FRANKLIN: You sure right. I prosper, not because of lawlessness, but because of enterprise and opportunity taken, where it is found. That is the essence of business is it not? You know what they say, about an ill wind, don't you, son?

JOJO: Yes sir, I know it well, shore 'nuff

FRANKLIN: . . . The proverb which states that most of them blow up a pretty fair silver lining after all is said and done. The foolhardy envision the colored and white shopping and dancing together in some parody of idealized 'equality'! If they are right, son, I guarendamntee you that will mean the end of this sweet little Cameo world. *(Lights crossfade with video)*

BUDDY: Man shouldn't try to make it by himself. Needs a help mate to keep him together. I got me a fine woman.

JOE: Yeah, one at every train station on the Sunset line.

FRANKLIN: I need to settle down get married again, ain't getting' no younger, you know. Need to grow me a garden, okra and tomatoes.

BUDDY: You?

FRANKLIN: That's what it's all about. The rest don't mean much. Good haircut and a shine, and somebody sweet to come home to. The one I should have married ran off to Chicago. If you ain't got trust, you ain't got nothing.

JOE: Well, they say there's still plenty of fish in the sea.

FRANKLIN: That's all well and good if you like seafood. *(Lights crossfade with video)*

Scene 6

(Characters speaking from video love scene excerpt of "The Thief of Baghdad" movie)

SHE: Are you a genie?

HE: No.

SHE: Why have you come?

HE: To find you.

SHE: Where have you come from?

HE: From the other side of time.

SHE: How long have you been searching?

HE: Since time began.

SHE: Now that you have found me, how long will you stay?

HE: Till the end of time.

SHE: You must go. It cannot be.

HE: Tomorrow then, here in your garden?

SHE: No, there is a gardener here who watches day and night, his name is Death. You mustn't come.

HE: Forbid me then.

SHE: I cannot forbid you.

HE: Tomorrow ...! *(He goes)*

SHE: And all tomorrows ...

(Fade to black)

Scene 7

(Lights up on street)

ROSE: I wasn't always the box-office girl at the Cameo, you know. No indeed. I used to work the evening shift at the San Antonio Laundry company. Made almost two-dollars a day. Working in the cotton-fields wasn't but a dollar and a half a week. So I was a happy woman, and stuff was sho' nuff cheap. But soon as that nine o'clock whistle blew, honey, I go home to my room at Miss Lula's rooming house on Olive Street, change my funky work clothes, get stylish, powder my nose, and sashay over to Commerce Street. First, I'd stop into the Chocolate Bar for a highball. Place was real dark, sweet and brown like the name, but sometimes just had too many nuts in it.

FRANKLIN: I had a little office on top of the barbershop years ago. Used to look out and see just about everything that was going on. Every train, Sunset Limited, coming in, going out. Used to be a fella' would sitting his wheel chair in front of the colored entrance of the S.P., called him Mr. Pete. Sat there, morning till night collecting pennies, nickels, ad dimes, with a little hand-made sign in his lap that said he lost his legs in World War II over in France. God bless 'em. Then we might see him on Saturday at the Avalon Grill buying beer with small change and dancing the Lindy Hop.

HELEN: Lord have mercy ... You mean he ... I thought that was the same man, but ... I just ...

ROSE: Everybody went to the Avalon. Blind, cripple, or crazy.

FRANKLIN: The Avalon always had the best dancers ... 'Cause they had the best music. Don Albert had the best band in Texas, bar none.

ROSE: I don't like to look at the streets too much. The more you look, the more you see ...

HELEN: Remember Big Mary and Little Mary? Folks used to say, "There go Big Mary and Little Mary going to the S.P. Station. Train must be coming in ... ?"

BILL: Were they related?

FRANKLIN: No, but they was sort of family.

BILL: Were they, you know, Ladies of the Evening?

HELEN: Yeah. And of the morning, noon, and night too, if you could afford it.

BILL: How'd they get those nick-names?

HELEN: Well, see ... Little Mary was sort of short and skinny you know, and Big Mary was, well ...

BILL: Big?

FRANKLIN: That's right, yes. And tall, too. They used to look out for each other all the time. Whenever you saw one, you saw the other ...

HELEN: Till Little Mary married this pimp from Dallas. He didn't like nothing about Big Mary.

FRANKLIN: After while, Big Mary sort of retired, so to speak. Took to drinking, looking bad. That was the end of that.

BILL: What happened to her?

HELEN: Heard she died a few years ago. Cirrhosis of the liver, folks said.

FRANKLIN: I believe it was worse; cirrhosis of the heart. Why you ask so many questions 'bout this old stuff anyway.

BILL: I'm a student. I want to tell this story ... For my dissertation ... my paper ...

FRANKLIN: Yeah, but why this old particular dying boom-town?

BILL: Do you know where Deep Elum is?

FRANKLIN: In Dallas, ain't it?

BILL: Or Sugartown, how about Bronzeville, or Washington Avenue?

FRANKLIN: Houston, Chicago. Do they have more in common than being black and enterprising?

BILL: They all are part of a pattern--once thriving social and business centers choked off by the noose of urban renewal. It's a government conspiracy.

ROSE: The hell you say . . . you think somebody had to plot and plan to keep us down?

FRANKLIN: Boy's got a point. Naturally a force of nature like the Black Spirit couldn't have been held in check for all these nasty years without some clear and purposeful effort to undermine our determination. Our accomplishments in arts and learning formed like a luminous black pearl around the persistent irritant of discrimination and malice. We are alas, victims of our own enterprising success. As we become a threat we have to be divided asunder. Freeway is as good a way as any. Once that Genie is out of the bottle, there's no going back in again. Always be careful what you be wishing for.

BILL: Hold on, you mean there are 'wishes' involved with this?

FRANKLIN: Don't be getting all excited. It's just an old traditional figure of speech. Like they say.

BILL: Yeah, but all the same . . . I didn't know.

(Train song plays. A well dressed woman, FLO, gets off the train and crosses into scene. She waves to ROSE, then sees JOJO and goes to him.)

FLO: Hey Joe, whatcha' know?

JOJO: Well as I live and breathe, look at what the Sunset Limited brought in. Thought you had went to Chicago for good, Miss Florinda Miller.

FLO: Don't try to get smart, Mr. Jojo. I had to come back and take care of some pressing personal concerns, like it was really your business . . .

JOJO: Girl like you always got a story to tell . . .

FLO: My life ain't hardly no mystery, baby, listen here.

(Sings)
    I'm just a small town girl
    With a big city body,
    And a one-way ticket home.
    If I had my way, I'd live
    Far from everybody
    All alone and on my own.
    But that is not my destiny,
    That's some other lucky woman, not me.

    I had to come back down south
    Back where the weather suits my clothes
    I walked around in Chicago till I done almost froze
    I walked around in Chicago, chile, till I done almost froze.

JOE: *(Sings)*
    I'm a small town boy who needs some big-city money
    And a way to break on through
    If I had my way, I'd make a million-dollar movie
    And bring it back home to you

    Wouldn't that be heavenly . . .
    That's some other lucky fella not me

FLO: *(Sings)*
    I had to come back down south
    Back where the weather suits my clothes
    I walked around in Chicago till I done almost froze
    I walked around in Chicago, chile, till I done almost froze.

JOE: *(Counterpoint sung simultaneously)*
    I have to go to where the brave go to misbehave
    And learn to save myself for something true—
    What in the world is that thing? Is it true love is it true fame
    Or just a name that sounds the same
    As the Blues?
    What in the world is that thing? Is it true love, is it true fame
    Or just a name that sounds the same
    As the Blues!

JOE: *(Speaking)* Bet Chicago ain't so bad if you got some love to keep you warm.

FLO: Uh huh, that's just the trouble . . . *(They exit)*

Scene 8

(HELEN, wearing an apron and holding a bowl of batter in house; BILL on the outside—they talk as in a trance to themselves rather than each other.)

HELEN: Joe! Joseph! Jo-Jo! Come on in here now, Oh Joe!

BILL: *(Answering her)* Are you a genie?

HELEN: No.

BILL: Why have you come?

HELEN: To find you.

BILL: Where have you come from?

HELEN: From the other side of town.

BILL: How long have you been searching?

HELEN: Since first thing this morning.

BILL: Now that you have found me, how long will you stay?

HELEN: Till I can't take it no more.

BILL: I must go.

HELEN: See you later alligator.

BILL: There is a crocodile who watches day and night, his name is Death.

HELEN: Are you trying to scare me?

BILL: *(To Joe)* Who's this lady?

JOE: My mother. She thinks you're me. She's calling.

BILL: She seems nice.

JOE: She was. There's something about when your mother calls you by name that makes you have to go. Don't know what it is—nobody does.

HELEN: Come on in now, Joe ...

JOE: Maybe it's the sound of it. A sound first heard while inside her very body, when she was all sound and sight and all in all.

HELEN: Joe's such a good child. Minds good and sweet manners too, from his little heart. Remembers everybody's birthday, sings on key, knows the names of flowers, trees and bugs and is good at hiding his wild side from the world.

JOE: *(Sings)*
> I won't go back to the windy city—
> the windy city is mighty pretty,
> but it ain't got what we got ...

HELEN: Lord how he loved them picture shows, too. That Cameo was like his second home. Would'a gone every day if I let him. It was so cute the way he would act out the little parts. I'd watch him out the kitchen window having a sword fight with his shadow or carrying on like Doris Day in *Calamity Jane,* or Maureen O'Hara in *Captain from Castille.* It bothered me at first that he was so drawn to the white lady movie star parts, but they was always the bravest women, and tough enough to threaten any man.

JOE: *(Sings)* Once! I had a secret love ...!

HELEN: You have to look at things from the proper angle or they don't make no sense at all ...

JOE: *(Sings)* That lived within the heart of me ...!

HELEN: He loved to drink Hippo sodawater, three or four bottles a day if you let him. Sodawater 'spose to rot the teeth, they say, but it just made my sweet boy's teeth shine brighter. The Cameo showed all kinds of movies. Some had black folks in them being pretty much themselves, like *Native Son* with Canada Lee or *The Well* about a town that has a race riot because of a stupid rumor. Sometimes there were all-black shows made in Hollywood for neighborhood theaters like the Cameo that then be-jeweled every black-bottom boom town ghetto-hood all over this rigidly segregated land of the free.

BILL: I'm all confused. It's getting sorta late . . .

JOE: What's the hurry? Don't you want to see the change that's coming?

BILL: Change? Better change my tape. From the look of things (winds blow) change is in the wind. *(Characters appear, turn and blow around.)*

Scene 9:
The Beauty Shop

(HELEN sits in chair getting her hair hot combed by FLO; two DANCERS nearby, one in dryer, or comb-out while the other assists during the following.)

HELEN: Thanks for helping me out, Flo. I couldn't get an appointment nowhere.

FLO: You know a colored woman can always get a job doing hair.

HELEN: Do me something pretty today, girl; my sweet boy's taking me to the Big Live Show at the Cameo tonight.

FLO: Sure enough. How 'bout a little curly flip with a French roll? I get to touch up o some of those Brown Skin Models' hair when they're in town. And that singer, Savannah Savoy. Folks say I kinda look like her.

HELEN: Yeah? I don't see it.

FLO: Me neither. Girl, I told you I used to fix Straight-Eight's hair, too. 'Fore she got sent to the penitentiary.

HELEN: Oooh! Weren't you scared?

(DANCER transforms into STRAIGHT-EIGHT during following and performs ritual funeral.)

FLO: Not one damn bit. She looked kinda scary that scar on her cheek like a crescent moon. Talked all gruff and gravely too, like Louis Armstrong with a bad cold.

HELEN: You so brave. I always get nervous around those types of women.

FLO: Why? You just don't understand it. Straight-Eight wasn't nothing but a natural woman, just like you and me.

HELEN: But wasn't she a stone cold killer? Kilt a whole bunch of people the way I hear it.

FLO: Straight Eight got blamed for everything but the Lindbergh baby. Yes she did kill a few people, but in her mind, she always had a good reason.

HELEN: Like what?

FLO: They lied on her or tried to cheat her some kind of way. She couldn't tolerate that. Sliced 'em up with a straight razor. That's how come she got that nickname.

HELEN: Cut 'em up with a razor. I can't even think about it.

FLO: 'Cept the one she stabbed with an ice-pick.

HELEN: Stop!

FLO: Yes, girl. Right through the eye. And that was somebody she loved. It paid to stay on Straight Eight's good side at all times. If she was your friend, she was there for you through thick and thicker. She wasn't just a cold blooded killer, by no means. This was a very compli- cated woman. Loved to gamble, shot craps on her knees just like any man. But she was a good Christian, too.

HELEN: Heard she went to church every Sunday.

FLO: That's right. Every Sunday when she was out of jail. She was a faithful member of the Church of God in Christ. Holiness. Got the warde to release her toward the end, so she could get baptized in the font before she died. Cancer.

HELEN: Do the Holiness water baptize?

FLO: Yes, chile. Dunk and dip and glory hallelujah. Everybody on Commerce Street came to that service, believe me.

HELEN: That must have been something. *(Pantomime of baptismal/ funeral; DANCERS with video insert.)*

FLO: Girl, the cars stretched all the way from Joske's corner to the graveyard on Pine Street. And plenty of folks mourned her too, men and women, black and white. She could be pretty scary, but that wasn't all she ws, you know . . . human beings can be very complicated.

HELEN: Where is she now tht we really need her?

FLO: Them that know ain't saying, and them that say, don't really know.

HELEN: Watch my ear, chile. Don't be rushing, now.

FLO: Here's some Vaseline baby. Don't want you to miss those Brown Skin Models.

Scene 10:
The Vaudeville Show

(Lights change to video projection of dancers in night club, etc. Buddy and Joe as Jimmy and Jocko.)

BUDDY as JIMMY: Ladies and Gentlemen. Welcome to the Cameo Theater, bringing you the finest in colored motion picture entertainment and tonight only presenting live on stage the world famous Bronze Peacock Revue! *(Cheers)* Featuring the fabulous Brown Skin Models, and the rhythmic stylings of Ronnie "Snakehips" Rogers and his band, the down home big city blues of the Montgomery Sisters, plus the queen of exotic dancers from the island of Zanzibar, the sensational La Movida! And starring our special guest, Bluebird recording artist, Miss Savannah Savoy. We're your masters of ceremonies for the evening. I'm Jimmy and this is my partner Jocko. Say hey to the people Jocko . . .

FRANKLIN as JOCKO: Hey people . . .

JIMMY: Before we start off the evening, we just want to remind you that tonight's show is for those folks between 18 and 80. That's, right. If you're under 18 you cain't understand it . . .

JOCKO: Uh huh, and if you over 79 your heart cain't stand it.

JIMMY: Let's start the fun with the fair brown-skinned beauty, direct from the island of Zanzibar, the luscious and lovely La Movida!

(DANCE does a shimmy-shuffle dance routine which ends with a flourish.)

JIMMY: How 'bout it! Let's hear it for 'em, folks. Think I could use a little Hadicol after that. Yessiree! Well, why you so quiet, Jocko? What you think about the exotic dancing?

JOCKO: I'm just thinking about Christmas.

JIMMY: Christmas?

JOCKO: Uh huh. Tell Santy Claus to leave her under my tree.

JIMMY: Jocko, you wouldn't know what to do with no woman.

JOCKO: Oh yeah? That's alright then. Don't need one. Just give me a half of one.

JIMMY: Half a woman? What you talking about man?

JOCKO: You heard me, just a half of one, that's right.

JIMMY: Can I have the other half?

JOCKO: Yeah, man, I ain't selfish, go on and take a half for yourself. What half you want?

JIMMY: What you mean, son?

JOCKO: The top half, or the bottom half?

JIMMY: The top half, man! Top half got all that pretty hair . . .

JOCKO: What you think my half is bald-headed?

JIMMY: Yeah, but mine got soft pretty lips to kiss and smack.

JOCKO: You think my half ain't got no lips?

JIMMY: Boy, you crazy! You don't know nothing about women do you?

JOCKO: Hey, folks, bet y'all ready for some real low-down barrel house blues, ain't ya? And here to deliver it up to you hot and heaping, direct from her sold out show at Chicago's Regal Theater, they are big, round, and velvet brown; the Montgomery Sisters!

(ROSE and HELEN sing as the Montgomery Sisters)

> Another flower on the wall, I was not born to be
> That's just not my style at all,

I got to D.A.N.C.E.—
And when I hear that slide-trombone,
responding to that   drum
Shut my mouth and take me home
And open wide, cause here I come—

If you wanna dance me,
You might as well romance me
You might as well take me back home
If you want to please me, squeeze me when you tease me
I'll let you be my chaperone—
I'll give a man a chance-
Just as long as he can dance-
If you want to dance me
You might as well romance me,
You might as well take me back home.

It thrills and chills me to my soul
When I feel that beat
Something crazy takes control
I get a fever in my feet
I lose my senses I admit
When I'm out on that floor
I don't ever want to quit
Please Mr. Bandleader, more, more, more!

If you wanna dance me,
You might as well romance me
You might as well take me back home
If you want to please me, squeeze me when you tease me
I'll let you be my chaperone—
I'll give a man a chance-
Just as long as he can dance-
If you want to dance me
You might as well romance me,
You might as well take me back home.

CODA:
I got no time for you unless you do the Susie Q
If you can't mess around you better get on out of town,

You sho 'nuff out of luck, if you cain't do the Hucklebuck
You might as well take me home---

JIMMY: Let's here it for 'em, folks, The Montgomery Sisters, two Queens beat a full house every time!

JOCKO: I knew you was gonna say that.

JIMMY: You didn't know no such thing.

JOCKO: Yes I did, too.

JIMMY: How you know?

JOCKO: 'Cause I can read your mind . . .

JIMMY: Read my what? You can't do no such thing.

JOCKO: Can too.

JIMMY: Prove it!

JOCKO: Alright, alright! *(Going into a trance)* I'm getting a message from the great beyond. Oh, it's a sad message. Very, very sad. Your daddy in Los Angeles, California is dead.

JIMMY: What? You don't know nothing. My daddy's alive and well and living in Harlem, ain't never even been to Los Angeles. What you got to say to that?

JOCKO: I say; your daddy in Los Angeles is dead. My voices don't never lie.

JIMMY: Man, you don't understand; I just talked long distance to my daddy 'bout a hour ago. Sounded real healthy and strong to me . . .

JOCKO: No, no, no, you don't understand. That Negro your mammy married is in Harlem, but your daddy is dead in California!

JIMMY: Man, get outta here talking about my mama!

JOCKO: And now . . . on with the show!

(FLO sings as Savannah with DANCERS)

For some strange reason
In every season I am blue—
Trying to get over

Trying to get over
Trying to get over you
I know you told me it's all over
I can't believe my four-leaf clover
Did not pull me through

Once I walked around with pride
Shoulders swinging side to side
Buick in Electro-Glide
But who am I now?

Who is this poor chile?
With a tear in her eye,
With a tear in her eye
Where there used to be a smile?
Oh, lost and all astray
Every since that day
Ever since that day
Since you went away

I was free and I was easy
Everybody tried to please me
My nights were light,
My days were breezy
But who am I now?

Everybody looked at me
Thank you ma'am. And how you be?
Lady of Philosophy
But who am I now?

Who is this poor chile?
With a tear in her eye,
With a tear in her eye
Where there used to be a smile?
Oh, lost and all astray
Ever since that day
Ever since that day
Since you went away

Once I walked around with pride
Shoulders swinging side to side

Buick in Electro-Glide
But who am I now?
For some strange reason
In every season I am blue—
Trying to get over
Trying to get over
Trying to get over you
I know you told me it's all over
I can't believe my four-leaf clover
Did not pull me through . . .

JOCKO: Let's hear it for her, the saddest woman in show business, Miss Savannah! *(Music up)* Come on, now people, let's get boogie-fied with the Brown Skin Models! Remember, look but please don't touch . . .! *(Dancers appear as BROWN SKIN MODELS and dance until fade out)*

Scene 11

(Aside)

BUDDY: Hollywood? Hollywood, California?

FRANKLIN: That's what his Mama told me . . . Said he had to go and be some kind of moving picture actor. Says that Hollywood is the only place . . .

BUDDY: . . . So, a colored movin' picture actor? Like Rochester or something?

FRANKLIN: More like Canada Lee or Rex Ingram.

BUDDY: Right, but look at Rex Ingram . . . One year he's playing the Lord God almighty in the Green Pastures, and the next year he's a giant genie flying through around in a big diaper. Neither one was what you would call a normal person.

FRANKLIN: That's Hollywood for you.

(Lights crossfade to BILL; interview continues)

BILL: I think I get it. There is no plot, no storyline—no taut suspense. Everything ends in ashes. Is that the best we can do?

JOE: The bet I can do. What about you? Can you dream without a drum? *(Joe gives drum to BILL.)* What can I tell you? Some folks are born to succeed. Others? Looks like they avoid it at all costs. We need a new beat, is all. An hombre's got to adapt to survive, transform to transcend, que no?

BILL: I have a wish coming. Are you a genie?

JOE: Not really.

BILL: Why have you come?

JOE: To find you.

BILL: Where have you come from?

JOE: From the other side of life.

BILL: How long have you been searching?

JOE: Since the world was made.

BILL: Now that you are here, how long will you stay?

JOE: Till the end.

BILL: I must go. I do not understand.

JOE: Forbid me then.

BILL: I cannot forbid you.

JOE: Come back tomorrow . . . ! *(He goes)*

BILL: If tomorrow ever comes.

(Fade to out)

Scene 12:
The Cameos

(Each character speaks to audience or more to self, rather than to each other.)

HELEN: My boy told me; 'Mama, I'm gone have to go now.'

BUDDY: *(Sings)*
>Train I ride—sixteen coaches long.
>When you hear that whistle blowing,
>I'll be traveling-o. Today's number is 866.

FLO: Yeah, I want to get married. Franklin asked me once, sure did. But while I was thinking it over, he commenced to acting all cold and salty. Finally I told me he was put out 'cause of me and JoJo. Shoot! Jojo is my friend. But a woman can't be friends with a man without folks thinking they courting. Tell the truth, I didn't mind him being jealous even under false pretences. How else you gonna know if your love is real? I had to go give my self a chance. Went to Chicago to think things over. Time flies in the Windy City. Still want to get married. That ain't no crime. Seem like all the husbands in Chicago was somebody else's. I can take care of myself when I have to. Always could.

ROSE: *(Sings)*
>This is my love song
>My melody for living
>My Little Cameo
>The perfect gift for giving--
>I like being me
>Been free since the day I was born.

>I love stormy weather
>I love my tight sweater
>But not every lady who's ever been born
>Is born to be Miss Lena Horne!

JOE: *(Sings)*
>I know I should speak now, I have something to say.
>Yes I should speak now. But this ain't the day
>Silence is golden
>But that's not my choice—
>I express myself in silence
>Cause I haven't found my voice.

>There should be singing now—
>Some beautiful song
>I hear it so clearly
>But something is wrong!

I've got to be strong
What if I sing it wrong?
What if I don't belong?
What if I don't really sing it?
What if I never sing it at all?

This is my love song
In old fashioned rhyme
My Cameo love song
In Commerce Street time

This is my love song
My Rondo in Blue
Quite sentimental
It's so sentimental
But I'm sentimental
Just like you . . .

FRANKLIN: People are such damn fools. When you get right down to it, no amount of cultural striving, technical advancement and social progress, can compensate for the sheer power of human stupidity. Pride. Greed. Vanity. Arrogance. The number of the day is 319. Con boys never complain of a sucker shortage. Good-game of three-card Monty gets going, and you have to beat the fools away with a stick. Charlatan roosters rule the roost. From the highest offices of church and state to the lowest low life judge and jury. If you don't believe me, read the papers.

HELEN: I stayed in town, because I wanted to. It's so beautiful here. Flowers, fiestas, and flowing waters. I had a chance to leave out of here, more than one or two. But truth to tell, I didn't want no more than this town had to give me. Had to raise my boy, then once he left, I had to stay so he'd have a home to come back to. A child's got to grow up and do what they need to do. But it scares me. You start worrying the day, they're born, and it never ends till one of you has laid that last burden down.

BUDDY: It's alright being a Pullman Porter. It's hard work, though; catering to white folks needs when that might not be your particular inclination at the time. But it's alright, answering "sir" when he says "boy," even if you old enough to be his daddy. Yeah, but it'll wear you out if you let it.

(Sings)

I got rambling, I got rambling on my mind . . .

(Speaks)

Then if you lucky, you get to work on the Jim Crow car, the colored folks car, where the tips wasn't nothing to speak of, but the food and conversation were always superior. Many a porter met his future wife while working the colored car. Get to put your best foot forward, be a real gentleman to these traveling ladies, and you never knew where it might lead.

(Sings)

Running the road means
Just to work and smile when you don't mean it—
From morning to midnight
Is to smile when you don't mean it,
After midnight, I retire
To my bunk to relax, to rest and rare back
All alone or with some sweetie like you,

While the miles roll by below,
I can roll you in my arms
Down below in my room
As the rhythm of the wheels
Keep time with my motion,
Let the miles roll by
Let the train roll on . . .

(Men join in)

While the miles roll by below,
I can roll you in my arms
Down below in my room
As the rhythm of the wheels
Keep time with my motion,
Let the miles roll by
Let the train roll on . . .

MR. FRANKLIN: Used to be you could tell a fool by the way he walked, even before he opened his fool mouth to confirm your suspicions. But to my way of thinking, foolishness has become the modern mode, and seems likes folks choose to behave foolishly even when they have another option. Out in California, they got something called a freeway. Mr. Rockefeller and Mr. Ford got together and decided we need it to sell more automobiles and gasoline. Freeway, is what they call it, but it ain't hardly free. It's us and our children who will pay, sooner rather than later. For fifty some years, we have built this neighborhood on the abandoned ashes of previous inhabitants. Built it, nursed it, polished and shined it to a fare thee well. Because we made it ourselves, we figure it can't be worth saving. Built your freeway in the sky. Ready to move on, move out and move along. Be careful with a fool. Someday he may get smart.

BILL: *(Remembering he is from another time)* This is 1965! What a great time to be black in America. President Johnson has pushed the leadership of the country to let the Bill of rights apply to all citizens only a hundred years after the Emancipation Proclamation. We have great black leaders too. Martin Luther King has become the conscience of the nation and woke up the world, and Malcolm X has just begun to speak and lead. Motown making millions, getting everybody to dance and sing along with funky poetry of the projects. At the same time, John Coltrane is expressing with fierce jazz our deepest and most complicated feelings! What a future we can build, now that the playing field has been leveled at last. We can finally come into our own. And this country can reach its full potential.

(Video)

HELEN: Joe always said, Mama, I'm gonna be a famous movie star, just you wait. Just like Sabu. I can do everything he can do plus I can sing like a bird. He worked hard at it to learning poems and things by heart and reciting them at lodge meetings and such. One day he up and told me . . .

JOE: *(To Mama)* I got to go, Mama, I got to try to answer my call. Ain't nothing for me here.

HELEN: *(To Joe)* But, son, Los Angeles is so far away. I just hate to think of you laying in some California gutter starving to death.

JOE: I won't starve to death, I promise. I'm gonna make it. If Canada Lee and Rex Ingram can make it in Hollywood, what's gonna stop me?

HELEN: I guess so, son. Just remember, you always got a home to come back to.

JOE: If Sabu can fly, then why shouldn't I try?

(Video of SABU and GENIE in the temple)

HELEN: *(Sings)*

> He was a dream of a son—not a minute's trouble—
> Everyone would look and smile and say
> "What a sweet looking one"—
> "What a sweet looking one"—
>
> A boy so pure of heart—
> So intelligent, so smart
> But now he's grown into a man
> Somewhat strange, something's changed
> In ways I'll never understand—
>
> But once it was
> The two of us against the world—
> And the world was not a place
> On who's top the two of us
> Could comfortably rest . . .
> But no matter we had each other
> And just like in the movies
> As the sun set in the sky
> The two of us found a way to get by—

HELEN: *(To audience)* When Joe came back, something had changed. Something happened in California. I never did know what it was exactly, but it was something bad. Joe wouldn't never tell me. Just say . . .

JOE: *(To Mama)* I'm tired Mama. I just got tired of trying.

HELEN: He still loved the picture shows, and loved to laugh. But his laugh was now bitter and sad. The pictures had changed and Commerce Street was changing, too. Everything was getting integrated by then. Folks didn't hardly come to the Cameo no more. Went to the drive-in movie, or the Majestic or the Woodlawn if they didn't have no car. Something broke that boy's heart alright enough. He never would tell me what it was. Now I'm dead and I'll never know.

And if I did know, tell the truth, I wouldn't care no more.

(ROSE and FLO join in and sing; Rose sings about Buddy, Flo about Franklin)

> The two of us against the world—
> And the world was not a place
> On who's top the two of us
> Could comfortably rest . . .
> But no matter we had each other
> And just like in the movies
> As the sun set in the sky
> The two of us found a way to get by—

BILL: They're going to tear it down. All of it. Nobody values it. Just ghetto land. Crime, punishment, exploit, condemn, move out move on. Develop, destroy, disenfranchise, disappeared, disappoint, dismiss, disillusion, and just plain diss'ed.

JOE: Don't rush off now. You gonna miss all the changes. Change is coming sure as shootin'. Play your drum.

BILL: What?

JOE: Just play it. For you, for me, for the change that's coming.

BILL: I hate change. *(Winds Blow. Video of changes in buildings, bright to dark and worn. Characters blow in, holding onto hats, etc.)* What's the point of it? Shouldn't there be a point? Just waves of people replacing each other over and over?

JOE: What is history? The story of the wandering of tribes. That's about it.

FRANKLIN: History is what is remembered. Isn't it?

ROSE: I don't know. I forget.

BILL: But why? Why did you come back here?

FLO: I came back because I was lonesome and tired.

JOE: I came back because I was tired of trying.

FLO: I came back because I was tired of being cold.

JOE: I came back because I was tired of being scared.

FLO: Talk is cheap. Men lie and then deny they are lying.

JOE: Men lie, and boys learn to ignore the truth.

FLO: Because I was hurt, and needed to heal . . .

JOE: Because I was used and not amused . . .

FLO: Because I failed to fly . . .

JOE: Because I failed to fly real high . . .

BOTH: I came back.

FLO: I like the sound of the traffic in the sky. Going somewhere.

JOE: I like the sound of the trains going by, been hearing it all my days.

Scene 13

(Drum rhythms under following; characters gathered all around the stage chanting)

FRANKLIN as ANNOUNCER: And now, ladies and gentlemen, the Cameo Theatre, home of the finest colored entertainment, proudly presents direct from its 'sold out' national tour, the world famous Urban Renewal Review!

ROSE: Have you heard? There's gonna be a big change . . .

BUDDY: Progress and a chance to urban-renew!

FLO: All for me?

ALL: All for you!

BUDDY: Gonna build an expressway in the sky—

ALL: Heading to the Northside. Passing us by . . .

JOE: On-Ramp located smack dab in the middle of Sam-Wo's . . .

ALL: Uh oh! Uh oh! Old Sam Wo has got to shoo fly shoo!

ROSE: Where's the off-ramp going to be at?

JOR: Negroes don't need no way in,
Just a way out to so-called opportunity . . .

FLO: Hey Mister Man, there's a problem with this plan.

BUDDY: It cuts the heart, it cuts the corner.
Commerce Street's gonna be a goner.

ALL: Commerce Street's gonna be a goner.

BUDDY: Just one little street don't matter none
To tell the truth, it's a potential slum—

ROSE: Sign, Sam sign—it's progress time.
Expressway waits on the dotted line

FRANKLIN: Once Sam sells, then the Church
around the corner—
Commerce Street's gonna be a goner.

ALL: Commerce Street's gonna be a goner.

FLO: Folks'll move out, businesses close—
Streets fall down like dominoes . . .

BILL: But what about the Cameo
Our very down home picture show?

JOE: You'll always have the top balcony at the Majestic
and the Empire downtown.
From there, the colored folks have a better view
Better than the white folks do.

ROSE: If certain people have their way
Pretty soon they'll come a day
You'll be able if you have the dough
To go to any damn picture show.

FRANKLIN: Ain't that what you want?
Assimilation? How else will we have
a unified nation?

FLO: Wait a minute Mr. Man—
Please don't you sell out—
Don't you give a damn?

ALL: Don't complain, don't complain

SAM: Don't make them declare, imminent domain!

ROSE: What's that? A new housing project!

FRANKLIN: It just means, that if you don't accept
the generous terms of their pitiful offer,
they'll write you a check for the cost of moving,
and then bring on the bulldozers!

FLO: Can they do that?

JOE: Yes, they can . . . imminent domain is the law of the land.

ALL: Imminent domain is the law of the land!
We got to go now, got to go
This is the end of the old Cameo Show!

Farewell good-bye, we got to go!
This is the end of the Cameo Show!

(Chanting ends)

BILL: That's it. Why doesn't somebody do something about this . . .

JOE: Why don't you?

BILL: I'm trying to . . . *(Beats drum wildly)* You've got to help me!

(Chanting begins again)

ROSE: Wait wait. Before it's too late.
Somebody's kicking at the pearly gate.

BUDDY: Somebody who knows right from wrong
Who ain't afraid to come on strong

JOE: Who ain't afraid to speak for me
Speak truth to greed
To plant a seed

HELEN: She's home at last
So open up the gate

ALL: Goodness Gracious
It's the late Straight-Eight

STRAIGHT-EIGHT: I'll cut your hear
    If you cut my corner—
    You're the one gonna be a goner
    This is purely guarantee
    If you mess with Commerce Street
    You mess with me!

(Chanting ends)

HELEN: We have to be smart. Smart enough to listen; nobody can be left out. We just can't afford it no more. The jailed, the free, the living, the dead, everybody needs to come to the table and have a seat.

ROSE: Blind, crippled . . .

FLO: Or crazy . . .

HELEN: You don't know. Nobody knows, what source, what force will get us from the dark night into the morning light . . .

BILL: I'm beginning. To wish. To work. To understand. *(Clicks off tape recorder) (Lights crossfade)*

Epilogue

(Tableaus take place in pools of light)

FLO: Are you a . . . ?

FRANKLIN: No.

ROSE: Why have you . . . ?

BUDDY: To find . . .

FLO: Where have you come from?

BILL: From the other side of . . .

JOE: How long have you been searching?

FRANKLIN: Since long ago and gone . . .

JOE: Now that you have found me, how long . . . ?

(Sings)
> Folks don't know
> They just don't know
> How far we had to come from
> How far we have to go

ROSE: *(Sings)*
> I came from New Orleans
> I'm back in San Antone
> But I'm going to Chicago
> Just as sure as you're born.
> Folks don't know
> They just don't know
> How far we had to come from
> How far we have to go

JOE: *(Sings)*
> I came from Alabam
> Outside of Birmingham
> But I'm going to San Antonio
> Just as fast as I can.

(Whispered)
> Without a drum
> The dreams won't come
> I might be crazy but
> I sho ain't dumb . . .
> Without a drum
> The dreams won't come
> I might be crazy but
> I sho ain't dumb . . .

THE END

From left: Bill Southerland and G.A. Johnson
in *Driving Wheel* (© *San Antonio Express-News*, 1992)

Driving Wheel

a memory play

Note: As You Read *Driving Wheel*...

Houston crafts *Driving Wheel* with a one-act structure of seven scenes set in a side yard in San Antonio in the mid-sixties. The action develops with the juxtaposition of the past and the present with several flashbacks in scenes three and four to earlier periods in the life of the approximately 30 year old central character, Joe Jr. This dramaturgical structuring device highlights the work as an autobiographical memory piece. It depicts the events primarily through the mind of Joe Jr. who returns home to confront his past, especially his conflicts with his now dead father about his homosexuality and desire to learn to drive. The significant memory of his relationship with his father is visually symbolized in the central image of an old American car on stage. Throughout the drama the car throws into relief the driving opportunity young Joe, Jr. was denied by his father, Joe Sr., even though ironically he called his son his "little Cadillac driver" when he was born. The car on stage also gives extra poignancy to the scenes with his father whose spirit returns to interact with him when he is asleep in the car. Father and son talk about the car, go driving, and discuss driving as a metaphor for life.

The image of the car on stage and the focus on the mental anguish of Joe, Jr. put this play in the expressionistic tradition of Elmer Rice's *Adding Machine* with its own oversized image--an adding machine on the stage. In addition, *Driving Wheel* is in the tradition of Tennessee William's *Glass Menagerie* in its flashbacks and focus on memory and Arthur Miller's *Death of a Salesman* in its focus on the action through the mind of the central character.

Finally, note that the discussions with his ghost father are surrealistic scenes juxtaposed with realistic scenes. A technique Houston identified as in the tradition of magical realism. In both the realistic and surrealistic scenes Houston highlights the African American Texan cultural milieu not only in references to the Avalon Grill, Wheatley High School, and collard greens but also through the music, e.g., Junior Parker's blues renditions of "Foxy Devil" and "Driving Wheel" and the vernacular language of the people on the East Side.

Maya Angelo encouraged Houston to write the play after he told her about his conflict with his father as a young man. Like many other American playwrights, e.g., Sam Shepard and Eugene O'Neill, Houston confronts his demons by exorcising them in drama.

Production Notes

Driving Wheel was first produced by the JumpStart Performance Co. in 1992 at the Carver Cultural Center in San Antonio, Texas with the following cast:

Cassandra Small	Clarice Ferguson
G.A. Johnson	Joe Ferguson Jr.
Bill Sutherland	Joe Ferguson Sr.
Kitty Williams	Maude Esther
Chuck Woodruff	Charles Harold
Kortney Wilson	Veronica

Director: Sterling Houston

Characters

Clarice Ferguson	A 50-ish widow
Joe Ferguson Jr.	A failed poet, her son; 30s
Joe Ferguson Sr.	The ghost of a father and husband
Maude Esther	Friend and neighbor; 40-ish
Charles Harold	Maude Esther's brother
Veronica	Maude Esther's 12-year-old

Setting:

San Antonio, Texas. In the side yard and porches of two modest frame houses; mid-1960.

ACT ONE

Scene 1

(At center in the middle of a side yard between two houses is an old American car with the hood open. DSR is MAUDE E.'s back stoop, and UL is the side-porch etc. of the FERGUSON house. JOE JR. is bent over leaning into car engine tinkering with a wrench. VERONICA is jumping rope DS, MAUDE is in her kitchen area dialing wall phone. Music up.)

CLARICE: Hello? Reverend? How do? This is Mrs. Ferguson. Clarice Ferguson, that's right. I joined your congregation about a year ago, right after I buried my husband . . . well, Greater Mount Calvary is such a big church now; its hard to remember everybody, I would think. Yes that's right, I work for the Board of Education, same as your wife, I work in the cafeteria at Douglass, where she's assistant principal. Yes, it sure is a small world, isn't it . . . *(shouts out door)* Turn it down please, Junior; I'm on the phone! *(JR. turns down car radio.)*

VERONICA: *(Rhyme-singing as she jumps rope)*
    Oh Mary Mack, Mack, Mack.
    All dressed in Black, Black, Black.
    With forty-four buttons, buttons, buttons;
    all down her back, back, back.

CLARICE: Beg pardon? Well, yes, I imagine you must be very busy and all, but I was wondering if you had a little time to see me soon, in private. Oh no; it ain't about me! I'm healthy and in my right mind, for the time being anyway. It's my son. My boy, Joseph Ferguson, Jr. I'm worried about him. No, he isn't sick, he's . . . he just doesn't have no get-up-and-go about him. Not that he's a trifling kind of person, not at all. Keeps his room neat as a pin, doesn't stay out all night worrying me to death like some boys do. But ever since my husband passed, Junior's been grieving worse than me, though he doesn't think I see it . . .

VERONICA: *(Rhyme-singing)* . . .
> She jumped so high, high, high;
> she touched the sky, sky, sky;
> and she didn't come back, back, back;
> 'til the fourth of July, ly, ly!

CLARICE: How's that Reverend? Oh, indeed? From who did you hear this? Oh, well, it doesn't really matter about that kind of talk anyway. It doesn't matter to me who he loves so long as he can love somebody. Crosses were sure enough made to bare, that's right. But that's not why I'm concerned about him, no, you see, he's gone and bought himself this old junk car, and my boy don't know nothing about cars. Nothing. I just can't understand it. It's odd when I think about it; his daddy drove a truck for forty years, but he would never teach that child to drive . . .

VERONICA: *(Rhyme-singing)*
> I asked my Mamma; for fifteen cents;
> to see the elephant jump the fence;
> he jumped so high; he touched the sky;
> he didn't come back 'til the Fourth of July . . . !

(She crosses to c. and watches JR.) What you doin'?

JOE JR.: Nothing. What you doin'?

MAUDE: *(Leans out her door)* Veronica! Leave that man alone and come in here and eat, girl!

VERONICA: O.K. Bye Junior. *(She goes into her house. M.E. comes down to JR.)*

MAUDE: You fixin' it all up, huh? JR.: Trying to.

MAUDE: Guess it's too late to get your money back . . .

JR.: I'm keeping it. I know it can go again. Sure has a good radio.

MAUDE: You know, Joe Jr., you never did strike me as real, what you call, mechanically inclined, more the artistic type. Don't get me wrong now, ain't nothing wrong with that. Where's your mamma?

JR.: She's in the house. On the phone, I think.

MAUDE: *(Calling out)* CLARICE! *(To JR.)* Now my older brother,

Charles Harold, he was always real mechanical; could fix damn near anything. *(Calling)* Oh CLARICE! *(To JR.)* He's coming over after while to play bid whist with us.

JR.: Charles Harold?

MAUDE: Unh huh. You want me to ask him to look at it for you?

JR.: O.K., sure.

MAUDE: 'Course, he ain't been inclined to do much of anything since his wife passed.

CLARICE: *(Comes out her door)* Maude Esther; hi girl. I thought that must be you hollering my name out. I was talking on the phone.

MAUDE: What you got smelling so good, chile?

CLARICE: Mustard greens.

MAUDE: Sister, them greens be sho' nuff talking up the neighborhood.

CLARICE: They're about ready. You want some?

MAUDE: No honey, I came to see if I could borrow your card table. You still got that old card table don't you?

CLARICE: Yeah, sure you can. Come on in. *(MAUDE goes past CLARICE into door.)* There it is, right there 'side the Frigidaire. Junior, don't you want some of these good old greens?

JR.: .Yeah, sure; thanks Mamma. I just want to try one more thing here.

CLARICE: Do you know what you're doing in there, son?

JR.: No. But I just might get lucky, you know. Can't have bad luck all the time. It's mathematically impossible.

CLARICE: Lord . . . ! I'll bring some on out to you. I know you must be hungry.

MAUDE: *(Enters carrying card table)* Thanks, sugar pie. See you about eight o'clock then.

CLARICE: Oh, I'll be there.

MAUDE: Don't forget what I said, now. Wear something cute. Bye Jr. Don't work too hard.

JR.: Bye Maude Esther. *(MAUDE goes into her house.)* What's she talking about; 'Wear something cute'? *(Scrapes his hand in engine)* Oww! Shit. Maybe I ought to take a little break.

CLARICE: Be right back. I'll bring you some greens and corncakes. *(She goes in.)*

JR.: Sounds delightful. Lunch al fresco! *(He crosses DR to water hose, turns it on and rinses his hands.)*

CAR RADIO: Folks, don't forget next Saturday night the Eastwood Country Club will present the fabulous Little Junior Parker, for two dynamic shows at nine and twelve midnight, and cats and kitties, you might want to get there early, cause when Junior Parker's in town the crowds do come 'round. He'll be singing all his hits backed by a twelve piece orchestra turning it every which-a-way but loose. So get on out to Eastwood, this Saturday, people and check out the one and only Little Junior Parker. It'll make you say "Oh, Yeah!" *(Music: "Foxy Devil")*

JR.: Bring me a beer, too, would you please!

CLARICE: *(Brings out a tray with two steaming bowls)* Sometimes food tastes better when you eat it outside. Why is that you think?

JR.: *(Takes food and beer)* I don't know. Probably reminds us of when we lived in the jungle.

CLARICE: I knew you'd have a answer. Is there anything my child don't know?

JR.: Good greens! *(He gulps food and beer.)* Ain't nothing like this in New York.

CLARICE: They got greens in New York; I know better. Drinking beer in the afternoon, is that a New York thing?

JR.: Don't worry about it. I can deal. What did you do woman, stick your big toe in these?

CLARICE: Quit now! You remind me of your daddy when you talk like that. He used to say I put my whole foot in them. Ha!

JR.: You really miss him, huh.

CLARICE: Like an arm yanked out of its socket. Dreamed about him, again last night. JR.: Did you?

CLARICE: It was a funny dream. He was all dressed up in a sandy colored lawn suit, spectator shoes, diamond tie pin. He always was a natural sport. For the longest time, he just stared at me, his eyes kinda turned down at the sides, like he was about to cry. Then he reached in his pocket, pulled something out and handed it to me in my hand. It was a little white baby shoe, kinda worn, scuffed on the sides. It felt real heavy in my hand, and when I turned it over, empty-ing it into other hand, out poured a shiny little pile of diamonds. It was the funniest thing. Been dead and gone for more than a year, and the man can't rest right for worrying about me. Poor thing.

JR.: You got me to worry about you now.

CLARICE: I know. That's what worries me. I mean, I'm worried about you. JR.: Me? Don't worry about me.

CLARICE: But what you gonna do? Don't you want to go back to New York?

JR.: No, Mamma. New York has changed, and I have too, boy have I.

CLARICE: You don't have to tell me if you don't want to. I just wish your daddy had lived to . . . I don't mean to talk about him all the time. I hate it when women talk about their dead husbands like they were the weather, or something everybody cared about.

JR.: I like when you talk about him. Seem like I hardly got to know him.

CLARICE: (Suddenly angry) That's because both of you were so damn hard-headed! (Calm) You were his heart, you know. His hope. Know what he said when he first laid eyes on you?

JR.: What?

CLARICE: He said 'Oh, here's my little Cadillac driver!' The mid-wife, old Mrs. Flores, had given you a little bath and was holding you up in her arms when he busted into the room, right off the road, truck motor still running he was so excited. Took one look at you and said 'Oh! Oh! Here's my little Cadillac driver! Gonna drive me all the way to California!'

JR.: What did he mean by that? California, huh?

CLARICE: It's the truth from here to heaven.

JR.: Then what happened?

CLARICE: Then you started to laugh. Yes! Laugh out loud. I don't mean no little baby grin, but a pure-dee laugh out loud. Sound like an old man.

JR.: Musta scared ya'll half to death.

CLARICE: Old Miz Flores had been a mid-wife since horse and buggy days, you know, and she swore up and down she'd never heard no new-born baby laugh like that. Cry yes; but LAUGH? Want some more greens? There's plenty. Help yourself. I've got to git, if I'm gonna make it to the beauty shop on time.

JR.: Getting your hair fixed just to play cards with Maude Esther 'nem? What's she cooking up for you tonight, some kind of blind date?

CLARICE: Nothing formal as that, I guarantee you. I'll be back in a little bit. *(She exits. Music up.)*

JR.: *(Returns to open hood, tinkers for a minute, gives up and takes a swig of his beer)* So I'm hardheaded? Was that it, Daddy? What kept you from giving me anything of yourself? You promised so much— then withheld fulfillment. Did you even try to understand? I'm a poet. Images and emotions run in my veins instead of blood. All you saw was softness, weakness. When I went to New York, you put barbed wire on top of the wall that had already grown between us. Maybe I am a fool. But I'm true to my foolishness. I'm sorry you were disappointed in me. But I'm not sorry for myself. Suffering is to the poet like high-octane fuel, allowing him to get to far away places with great speed and efficiency. *(He drains beer can, opens front door of car and lies down. DRIVING WHEEL music up. JR. sleeps as lights change to evening. Light inside car pops on as JOE SR. rises from backseat. He gets out of car and smiles at JR. as lights and music fade to OUT.)*

Scene 2

(Sound of insects and birds singing. Lights up on JR. tinkering with engine as before. JOE SR. stands near him. The light is dreamy and rich with shafts of sun colors.)

JOE SR.: Well, oh well! Went and bought yourself an automobile did you!

JOE JR.: That's right.

JOE SR.: That's good, that's good. A man without an automobile is a piss poor fella, and that's for damn sure. How much she cost you?

JR.: Hundred dollars. As is.

SR.: Hundred dollars cash? Where'd you get that kind of money, son.

JR.: Wasn't that hard really. Cutting grass, throwing the paper . . . whatever. I gave half to Mamma and saved the other half, till I had enough. No big thing.

SR.: Well ain't you something. Yessir, a fella without a car ain't about much of nothing. Couldn't be. It's a matter of time and distance. If you're walking, you see, you spend all your time getting where you going, and once you get there, if it turns out to be someplace you don't really want to be, you got to wait for the bus driver, or some other driver to drive you, before you can get the hell on out.

JR.: I guess you're right.

SR.: And Shoot! In this town, folks waiting at the bus stop can die of frostbite in the wintertime and sunstroke in the summer. God bless the child that's got his own car! Is it running?

JR.: I drove it over here yesterday, but when I tried to start it up again, nothing happened.

SR.: You mean it wouldn't turn over?

JR.: It wouldn't do nothing, not even click.

SR.: Get in and crank it up.

JR.: *(Gets in car and tries the ignition.)* See? Nothing. And the battery was just recharged. I recharged it myself.

SR.: No, it ain't your battery.

JR.: *(After a pause)* So what do you think it is? The starter?

SR.: *(Slides under car. He gets back up, dusting off his hands.)* What you have here, son, is a solenoid problem.

JR.: A solenoid problem. You mind telling me what the hell a solenoid is?

SR.: A solenoid, you see, is this little whatchamadoo that fits into the starter. If the solenoid goes out, then the starter don't start, and there you sit.

JR.: So here I sit; so what can I do? Can I fix it?

SR.: It can't be fixed; it's got to be replaced. Don't suppose you got a spare one around here.

JR.: Right.

SR.: Got a little screwdriver? A little one?

JR.: Yeah. *(Gets tool from trunk.)* What's up?

SR.: I think I can make you a temporary adjustment. Till you can get it replaced. *(He slides under car.)* You know Junior, ain't nothing to taking care of no car. Just simple easy things'll add five or ten years to the life of any automobile. Even this old tank.

JR.: Simple like what?

SR.: Well the main thing is to always check your fluid levels. 'Specially your oil. Change it more often than you're supposed to. I'm serious. If you pull out that dipstick and the fluid that drips off looks more like black-strap molasses than cane syrup, then it's time for an oil change. *(He gets back up.)* Get in and try it now.

JR.: *(Car cranks without turning over)* Sounds like it wants to start.

SR.: It sure wants to, don't it. Try it again. It wouldn't hurt to have these cables replaced. They split in a few places. Means big trouble down the line. . . . What it really comes down to is: pretty much you take care of it; it'll take care of you, whether it's a horse, an automobile, or a child for that matter.

JR.: What do you mean by that exactly?

SR.: Don't exactly mean anything by it other than just saying it cause it's true.

JR.: Truth has many faces.

SR.: More like different expressions on the same face. Know what I mean?

JR.: It's too late for all that. Why did you come back to haunt me? It's over. I don't need you.

SR.: Yeah. But maybe I need you. You don't seem real surprised to see me.

JR.: The last time you surprised me was when I was fifteen, and one of your friends told you I was 'like that'; and you realized that I was one of them, that I was 'funny' as you called it, not daring to say the word 'gay'. You slapped me across the face with the back of your hand, remember? As though my queerness was somehow an insult to your fatherhood. That you were the injured party, not me.

SR.: I didn't come back to argue all that up again. I can't change who I am anymore than you can. But now that I'm dead, I found my voice at last. Do you hear me? Do you hear what I'm trying to say to you?

JR.: I'm trying to hear. I'm starting to hear.

SR.: Good. Got any gasoline?

JR.: Half a can in the trunk.

SR.: Bring it here and let me show you something. Now, take a little of that gas and drip it right down the middle of that carburetor, there; not too much, now. Yeah. Alright, go on try to start it now.

JR.: *(Cranks engine and car starts. He guns the motor.)* Alright!

SR.: Ha ha! Come on then let's take it for a drive around the block. There's a couple'a'more things I got to tell you.

(They drive off as lights fade to out. Music up.)

Scene 3

(Music up. Lights up on MAUDE, in her window on telephone.)

MAUDE: . . . Yes girl, you know I got to go out to Eastwood and see Little Jr. Parker. Us married women got to take our thrills when we can get 'em. What you mean 'your husband won't let you,' Don't tell him. You gonna be with me, how much trouble can you get into? What? No. I do not think Little Junior Parker is ugly; even if that nose is kinda spread all across his face. Girl, with a voice like that, he can come over here and be ugly on me any time! What you Say! Ha! Well, if you can't go, you just CANT, that's that. Maybe I can get my neighbor to go with me. Clarice. You know Clarice. Used to be Clarice Hawkins. Went to Wheatley with us long years ago. That's the one! Married Joe Ferguson, had a son that went off to New York and got into the Life. What you mean 'What life?' The Gay Life, girl. I swear, sometimes you are so country. He's a sweet boy, but he got a hard way to go. His daddy was so hard on him when he was coming up. You know the kind . . .

(Lights crossfade to Ferguson area—flashback to the past)

CLARICE: Don't be so hard on him Joe; he didn't mean nothing! Please!

SR.: Get out of my way! (JOE SR. pushes JR. and he falls.)

CLARICE: He's sick. Can't you see he's sick?

SR.: Sick hell! He's drunk! You got the nerve to come in here falling down drunk, as hard as I work to get some respect for this family, and you come disgracing yourself!

JR.: I didn't mean . . . I . . . !

SR.: You had a wreck, didn't you! After I told you not to drive . . . You and that boy Buddy driving around in his Daddy's car like a couple of common hoods. You still not too big for me to take my belt off to your ass!

CLARICE: Joseph don't! You got all the neighbors looking out their windows!

SR.: Let 'em look! You think they didn't see the police car pull up and bring this no account to my front door?

JR.: I don't care let'em see ... let 'em see everything ...!

CLARICE: You only got another month till graduation! You can do what you want! Don't mess it up now, come on in the house and wash your face, son.

JR.: *(After a pause JR. becomes nauseous, holds his mouth and runs inside.)*

CLARICE: JUNIOR! *(She follows him in.)*

SR.: *(Unfastens his belt, pulling it off during following.)* Don't you vomit on that floor! Goddammit, I'm gone make you lick it up! *(He goes in. Lights crossfade to MAUDE.)*

(Return to present)

MAUDE: ... Yeah, girl; I don't know why people make problems out of little things that just keep life from being boring. Let me get off this phone, I got company coming directly, and haven't started cleaning this place. See you later, alligator.

Scene 4

(Music up as lights crossfade to CLARICE getting her hair done.)

CLARICE: I met Joseph Ferguson when I was twenty years old, and we were married within a year. But Joseph wasn't my first husband, no indeed. When we met, I had been the widow Hawkins for two years, having married old Rev. Hawkins when I wasn't nothing but seventeen. He had a heart attack about a year later, during an exceptionally vigorous usher board meeting. People tried to say I caused his heart attack, you know how people talk, but I wasn't nowhere near him when it happened. Then Joseph Ferguson began to court me, as gently as you please.

We both sang in the choir which was one of the only things I liked about Rev. Hawkin's church. Joe took me out on my first date. We went dancing at the Avalon Grill, to a real live band and everything. We got married at the court house, and Junior was born nine months later to the day. Joseph was a good provider. Made a pretty good wage for a colored man back then. Worked for the same people,

Larkins Furniture Co, driving a truck for almost thirty years. He was a man who actually liked grocery shopping; knew where all the bargains were. Funny the things you think about. He never cared too much for white folks, his dislike made bitter by fear. That's how they are,' he'd say, after reading about some devilishness done to the colored by the white. That's just how they are!' Like he could bare their cruelty if it was natural, and not inhuman like it always seems. He wasn't in favor of integration and all that. Him and Junior just argued about it all the time. *(Lights crossfade to DS)*

(Return to past)

SR.: Aw you don't know nothing about white people, nothing! None of you young ones know anything about nothing, but you think you know everything there is to know.

JR.: You all the time worrying about white folks. The hell with them.

SR.: To hell with them? It's fine to talk about to hell with them when hell is where they would like to see us all.

JR.: There's good ones and bad, just like colored.

SR.: But good or bad, he owns the whole pie! How you come talking about getting your piece of the pie, when he owns the whole pie; hell, the whole bakery. White man's only use for the nigger is just that; to use him. Take what you got and give you nothing to show for it. My grandmama was born a slave over in Guadalupe county; it's on the record at the courthouse. Not her birth, mind you; but the fact that she was her master's property

JR.: Slavery was a long time ago, Daddy. We got Mr. Thurgood Marshall now. Brown versus Board of Education.

SR.: You think if he lets you in his schools, he'll let you in his world? All you gonna do is loose your own Negro schools. Colleges. Look at Commerce Street down by the S.R Station. We got blocks of colored business, restaurants, hotels, tailor shops, barbershops, a picture show; it'll all get wiped out; all we worked for, fighting up hill every step, is just gonna get washed away in a wave of "brotherhood"!

JR.: That's why I can't wait to get out of this town! Progress don't mean nothing around here.

SR.: I'll tell you what means something to me. Having you respect what I say to you as much as you do those white teachers at that white school!

(Lights crossfade to CLARICE in present)

CLARICE: *(She is dressing to go out.)* He had a bad temper. But worse than his fussing, was his silence. Days might go by and you wouldn't know what had made him mad; just that his mouth was all stuck out again about something. I learned to deal with it, but Junior would take it personally.

(Crossfade to past)

JR.: What? What did I do? I can't say I'm sorry, if I don't know what I did.

SR.: *(After a pause)* . . . Stay away from that boy Buddy, he's no good and I don't want him coming over here no more. You hear me?

JR.: Why? What did he do to you?

SR.: Don't get smart. You know what you need to know.

JR.: *(Sighs in frustration as SR. exits.)* *(Lights cross fade to card game area)*

(Return to present)

CLARICE: We lived a pretty good life, the three of us. Always paid the rent, kept food in the house. Then Joe Jr. quit college and ran off to New York to find himself, as he put it. Then Joseph took sick and after a few years, died on me; just like Reverend Hawkins had done so many years before. Except I never loved Reverend Hawkins, and I didn't have to watch him die, day by day. Joe was eaten alive by cancer and regret, until the pain of both combined can't even be killed by dope. Then death comes like a mercy. But death isn't really the end of anything; is it? Not the end of anything at all.

MAUDE: *(After a pause)* Come on, Clarice! It's your play, girl.

CLARICE: Oh, excuse me; I kinda drifted off didn't I. *(She plays a card.)*

MAUDE: No, sugar; clubs is trumps. Ain't you got no hearts?

CLARICE: I'm sorry. You'd think I never played cards before.

CHARLES HAROLD: That's alright partner; we can still whup 'em.

VERONICA: How come I have to play cards? *(No reply)* How come Mama?

MAUDE: Because your daddy ticked me off royally, so I had to tell him about himself. He left out of here bookin' knowing that I had invited company to play cards, and went off somewhere in the streets to suck his thumb, I expect.

VERONICA: I still don't see why I have to.

MAUDE: Because I said so. Now be still and play girl. I don't want to have to wear you out in front of company. *(To CLARICE)* Just getting to be so FAST. You lucky you never had no little girl.

VERONICA: I got to be fast to keep up with my 1965 CLASS!

MAUDE: Girl, I'm going to knock the naps out of your big head, if you don't quit.

CHARLES: Maybe we shouldn't play cards right now, Maude Esther . . .

MAUDE: No indeed! I invited Clarice over here to play cards, and we are going to play!

CLARICE: It's O.K. by me, whatever we do. It's nice to get out of my house, even if it is just next door.

MAUDE: Next Saturday night is Little Junior Parker at Eastwood. Come on go with us, Clarice. All you do is work and go to church. Don't you think that'd be what's happening? You come to, brother-mine . . .

CHARLES: Yeah, if Clarice would be kind enough . . .

CLARICE: Why not? I haven't been out to Eastwood since Jr. was little.

VERONICA: Junior is a punk.

MAUDE: Girl, I'm gonna have to kill you. *(Raises her hand as if to strike; VERONICA gets up to dodge her.)*

VERONICA: Junior is a sissy punk! Junior is a sissy punk! *(VERONICA runs off as MAUDE rises.)*

MAUDE: Veronica! Lord, I swear, I don't know where she gets it. Veronica! Girl, you better answer me when I call you. Ya'll excuse me, please. *(Exits)*

CLARICE: *(After a pause)* You have any children, Charles Harold?

CHARLES: Me? Oh yes. Four girls. All married and moved. I've got nine grandbabies. Believe that? A young fella like me?

CLARICE: That's nice.

CHARLES: And you?

CLARICE: What? Oh; just the one. Son. Still not married. He's home with me.

CHARLES. Well, shoot! I got enough grand kids to spare you a couple, till he comes through.

CLARICE: That's mighty nice of you. You seem such a kind person.

CHARLES: Kind enough, when folks let me. But I'm going to have to fuss at my sister, for keeping you a secret for so long ...

CLARICE: You wouldn't be trying to flirt with me now, would you sir?

CHARLES: I'm surprised I still remember how. It doesn't offend you does it? I know how it is with that grief situation. My wife passed two years ago this April. Sugar diabetes. Suffered with it a long time, you know how it is.

CLARICE: I'm sorry to say I do.

CHARLES: But that grief situation, that mourning thing, it's on going, everyday. Some days it'll hit you hard, but most times it's like a low humming noise in the background. It doesn't ever really go away.

CLARICE: I like the way you put that. You have a nice way with words. My son is a poet. Had his poems printed in a book when he was up in New York. I'll show it to you sometime.

CHARLES: I'd like that. We have some mighty great Negro poets in this country you know. Countee Cullen, Langston Hughes ... Do you like poetry?

CLARICE: I don't know much about it. But I like Junior's. Even if I don't always understand it. When he was in high school, he would stay in his room for hours writing and reading. Come home, eat, and then I might not see him till the next morning. You know, when I child is gifted he's often misunderstood. He'd always be getting his feelings hurt, by some teacher or some jealous classmate. And him and his daddy didn't get along. So he just felt safer in that room with the door closed, playing the radio and writing his poems, long after his daddy and I had gone to bed.

(Crossfade to JR. in the past sitting at desk. Music up. JR. is typing the last section of a poem into a portable typewriter. A cigarette curls up from the ashtray. He pulls paper from typewriter, and begins to read.)

Searching for Bethlehem in the stormy desert
I stumbled upon Mecca in the form of a smooth black tower.
It vibrates at my touch
Reproducing the deep brown cello music
Of my mother's voice.
I bless myself for being blessed in the twisted metal face
Of hope shattered like headlights in head-on crashes.
I declare myself to be a thing as complete as an idea in the mind
Of some unique and cunning ancient god,
Containing all things essential for a journey in this world
Of multiple realities
Of sacred laughter and
Profane tears.

(Return to present. Lights crossfade to card game area. VERONICA and MAUDE enter.)

MAUDE: Veronica has something to tell ya'll. Go on, now.

VERONICA: I apologize for being so rude and sassy ...

MAUDE: And what else ... I

VERONICA: . . . And I promise not to do it no more.

MAUDE: ANY more.

VERONICA: Anymore.

MAUDE: That's fine. Now you may be excused to do your home-work, young lady. *(VERONICA exits.)* Lord, I don't know what I'm going to do with that girl.

CLARICE: I know she doesn't mean any harm. She's just a child.

MAUDE: I am so sorry this evening turned out this way. I wanted everything to be so nice . . .

CHARLES: Plans can be like that sister; don't be worrying about it too much. I got to meet this nice lady, didn't I? And we going to Eastwood Saturday night ain't we?

CLARICE: Sure, we going; a real date, that's right.

CHARLES: Say! How 'bout if I drive us all up to the Dairy Queen for a malted milk! Huh? What do you say?

VERONICA: Bring me a chocolate!

MAUDE: You better get that lesson. Don't make me come back in there.

CHARLES: How about it, Clarice? Wouldn't a nice malted milk hit the spot?

CLARICE: That would cool me down a bit. So warm this evening.

MAUDE: But we don't want you to cool off too much, do we Brother.

CHARLES: Well no; I reckon we don't.

Scene 5

(Current time—mid-sixties. Music Up. Lights up as car comes to center. JR. and SR. are driving through the neighborhood.)

SR.: Look out! Did you see that Jackass! *(Shaking his fist.)* Asshole! Ya see, that's one of many benefits of driving around in traffic; you get to chastise transgressors on the spot.

JR.: I don't think they heard you. I hope not.

SR.: That light's getting ready to change. Get ready to stop now . . .

JR.: Wow, dad are you psychic too? Is that one of the side-effects of being dead?

SR.: Shoot! That's nothing, minor stuff. I could fly if I took the notion to do so. Take off and fly right through the air. But I wouldn't want to scare you. You might loose control.

JR.: Thanks. And try not to burst into flames, if you can help it.

SR.: Son, it just wouldn't be right if I didn't tell you something else, something that's not easy for me to say . . .

JR.: Uh oh. Maybe I should pull over.

SR.: There's a price. A price you pay for driving. And the price is always going up. Not down.

JR.: I guess that's fair. Balance in all things, they say.

SR.: For some, having a car is nothing short of a continuous heart-ache. Just keeping it running right is a constant challenge. No sooner you get your brakes done, buy a new set of tires, then the water pump goes out and the transmission ain't acting right.

JR.: I suppose any old car would be . . .

SR.: That's just it! Not just old ones; the new ones too. And all of them burn gas and eat up insurance money. It's the price you pay, you understand; the PRICE!

JR.: Yeah, I hear what you're saying. A car is like a family: great to have around when you need 'em, but always needing something you don't want to give.

SR.: Let me tell you something; there's worse things than being needed. Even by a machine. Look out! Don't you see that stop sign? Don't trust the other driver to see you.

JR.: I see the stop sign. It's a four-way stop sign.

SR.: See, *(Looking out window)* that's just what I'm talking about. That was a white lady driving, and white ladies don't necessarily believe that stop signs apply to them.

JR.: So, how you handling the white folks on the other side? Don't tell me you got integrated at last!

SR.: It ain't nothing like that. Ain't no white folks over there.

JR.: What?

SR.: No black folks either; not exactly, you see . ... it's kinda hard to explain. Plus, I ain't exactly been over to the other side, not all the way over. Not yet.

JR.: Wow, I hope I remember this when I wake up.

SR.: Turn right here, and we'll be right back home.

JR.: This IS my dream, isn't it? Not yours.

SR.: All of it's a dream, Joseph, yours, mine, and all the rest of it. That's what makes it so funny. *(Starts to laugh)* So damn funny.

JR.: What's funny?

SR.: All of it! People crying at funerals! Ha! HA! Saying, 'I'll love you forever!' HA! HA! HA! Talking about 'Peace On Earth!!' Peace in the valley! *(calming down)* Peace in the valley, some day. *(Lights crossfade)* Home, home again. That's enough driving for me for a while. Enough sightseeing, too . . . Things change so fast. Too fast.

JR.: Has it really changed that much?

SR.: I almost didn't recognize it. Commerce Street used to be so alive! I guess I was too, long years ago.

JR.: How did I do? Driving pretty good huh?

SR.: You did alright, for a beginner.

JR.: It's hard for you to give me a compliment, isn't it? Why you always have to be the hard one.

SR.: Ha! You think I'm hard? Now, my papa, Old man Wilson, he was a sonofabitch. Always angry about something; with his mouth all stuck out. Couldn't please him if you saved his life. But I forgave him his licks and hurtful words. Even the way he talked to my mamma; I forgave him.

JR.: You want me to say I forgive you?

SR.: Listen, son. The most important thing about driving a car, the one thing above all else; you must always do. Look out for the other fella.

JR.: Look both ways at a stop sign?

SR.: Promise me you will. Every time.

JR.: O.K. I promise.

SR.: 'Cause sure as you're born, no matter how fine your driving is, how razor sharp your responses are, here comes some sucker late for work, or drunk, runs a stop sign and hits you broadside. Next thing you know, you waiting for the bus again.

JR.: Why are you telling me all this now? For ten years you hardly had anything to say to me.

SR.: I wanted to. I wanted to talk. Told myself I'd wait till I saw you again. Wait till you came home. But when I finally did see you again, I couldn't concentrate on anything but my pain. There you were. My fine boy. Standing by my hospital bed. If I could have made a sound I wouldn't have known what to say. And when I looked in your eyes, all I could see looking back at me was my own sick pain, magnified by yours. Cancer had been feasting on my insides for months, like every day was Thanksgiving. But it wasn't till I saw you again that I knew I was really going to die.

JR.: I never hated you.

SR.: You didn't even come to my funeral.

JR.: I couldn't bring myself to go. I heard the undertaker stuffed cotton in your cheeks to make you look more natural. I couldn't bear to see it.

SR.: Old Franklin Brothers did a hell of a nice job. Very artistic! You should'a seen it.

JR.: Maybe I should have.

SR.: *(Rooster crows)* Look, I can't be hanging around here much longer. It's good you stayed around here to help your mamma some; but you got to start thinking about yourself. I know you want to be moving on someday soon.

JR.: I did go to the graveyard though, and I watched them lower you into the ground. Watched the yellow chrysanthemum petals fall onto your coffin lid. Ashes and dust. I wanted to scream. Scream in frustration and rage. But mamma saw it building up in my throat. She grabbed me by the arm, saying: 'No, not here. Don't embarrass us. Be strong. Scream later.' But later never came, and neither have the tears.

SR.: *(Pulls stickpin from his tie.)* Here. I want you to have this old horseshoe pin. Ain't but one of the diamonds real. I forget which one. You take it now. It was pretty lucky for me, when all's said and done. Go on, take it. Luck to me now is like water to a drowning man.

JR.: I can't take that. It's part of you. Besides, you already gave me something of yourself. *(He pats car.)*

SR.: I'm glad about that, son; and you've given me a way to get on over *(SR. vanishes as dogs bark. Lights out.)*

Scene 6

(Current time, present, mid-sixties.) (Lights up. JR. is sleeping inside car with his feet out the open car door. It is late evening. Crickets and distant music. VERONICA comes out carrying garbage.)

VERONICA: Here Kitty-Kitty-Kitty. *(She notices JR's feet out car window and goes to investigate. She touches his foot. He wakes.)* Mamma! Miss Clarice! Junior done passed out drunk!

(CLARICE comes out followed by MAUDE and CHARLES)

CLARICE: Junior?! What in the world? You'll catch your death of cold out here in this night air.

JR.: What . . . ? I'm not cold.

MAUDE: *(Picks up beer can)* Man, you got your head that bad on one can of beer? Well, you know your daddy couldn't hold his liquor neither.

CLARICE: Maude Esther! Don't speak ill of the dead.

JR.: I don't remember falling asleep.

VERONICA: Take me for a ride when you get sober; if this old thing can run.

CHARLES: Is this the old car you wanted me to look at?

MAUDE: Yes! Junior, this is my brother Charles Harold. You believe he paid a hundred dollars for this pile of junk.

CHARLES: How you doin'? *(Looks under car hood)* Let me take a look. It don't look that bad to me. Give it a crank. *(Car engine starts; motor guns.)* Ain't nothing wrong with that motor.

CLARICE: You fixed it!

JR.: Yeah, how 'bout that. *(Gets out of car)*

VERONICA: Take us for a ride right now, Junior! *(VERONICA gets in car and bounces on front seat.)* Ouch! Something bit me! Oh look! it's an old pin. Finders keepers, losers weepers! *(She gets out of car and runs around.)*

CLARICE: Let me see that! *(VERONICA gives pin to her.)* That's what I thought; a diamond horseshoe!

CHARLES: Must have been left by a previous driver.

CLARICE: It belongs to Junior now. Doesn't it belong to you now, Junior?

JR.: By rights, I guess it does. *(Lights dim to out)*

Scene 7

Epilogue

(A few weeks later. JR. is polishing car. MAUDE attends grill, as VERONICA sets paper plates.)

VERONICA: When we gonna eat, Mamma? I'm hungry.

MAUDE: Soon as Charles Harold and Clarice get here. Go get yourself some potato salad out of the ice box if you're hungry. *(VERONICA goes in.)* I wonder what's keeping those two.

JR.: It's good to see them getting along so well; Mamma needs to get out more.

MAUDE: YOU the one needs to get out. How come you didn't go to Eastwood with us? It was fun,

JR.: Mamma said she had a good time.

MAUDE: Honey, yes! Got right into the swing. You know that Little Junior Parker really puts on a show. Had sweat soaking clean through his silver shark-skin suit! Ha! All the women just hollering, and Clarice was right there hollering with 'em!

JR.: Alright!

MAUDE: Hey! I heard you got accepted at college! University of California hey, hey! I hear they a pretty fast bunch out there.

JR.: I can deal with it. I got to.

MAUDE: They really gave you a scholarship for making up poems?

JR.: Somebody must think they're pretty good.

MAUDE: I know Clarice is proud. She's sure gonna be lonesome with you gone.

(CLARICE and CHARLES enter)

CHARLES: Hope ya'll saved us some barbecue.

MAUDE: Hey! We been waiting for you.

CLARICE: We lost track of the time walking around downtown.

MAUDE: Veronica, bring out the potato salad and Kool Aid.

JR.: What's happening downtown?

CLARICE: We just window shopped. I like looking in Joske's windows at all those nice clothes I can't afford. *(VERONICA comes out with salad, etc.)*

CHARLES: But that's just a temporary situation. Junior's going off to be a famous writer, get rich, and bring it all back home to you. Ain't that right?

JR.: I don't know. Not many poets get rich, Charles.

VERONICA: You gonna drive that old car all the way to California?

JR.: Uh huh. New tires, tuned-up and ready to hit the road . . .

MAUDE: That car ain't no older than you, miss smartness; both of ya'll got a few good years left.

CLARICE: Junior, you won't try to drive all night, will you? Pull over side the road and sleep when you get tired. Promise me.

JR.: Oh yeah; I intend to take my time.

CLARICE: Your Daddy would be so proud of you; going off on your own. He knew you were born to drive yourself to whatever life holds for you. I knew too; ever since you were little, that day at Playland Park . . .

JR.: I almost forgot about that. Fourth of July, wasn't it?

CLARICE: That's right! Junior wasn't nothing but five or six. Well, bless his heart, he heard this announcement on the radio, where the radio man had said they here having this big old celebration over at Playland Park for the Fourth of July, which it was that day, with fireworks and the army band and all, and everybody was welcome. He stressed that word: Everybody. Now, who was I to tell this child he wasn't somebody? He was bound and determined to go to Playland Park to watch the fireworks along with everybody else who was welcomed that day. Now, remember this was in the late forties. Folks around here still lived pretty much the way they had since emancipation. Still had 'Colored only' or 'Whites only' signs on everything from restaurants to toilets. Yeah, toilets! Like their shit was too good to go down with ours. Yes Lord, Jim Crow was in full flight, and not too many of us were acting up about it in those days, lynching was not unheard of. So for us to go to Playland Park on a day we were not welcome was more than a notion. But there was no denying that boy. So sure of himself; nothing would do him but to go. So I took a deep breath, talked to God a minute, and we went on over there. It was about a half an hour away on the bus-line. He just couldn't stop talking all the way over; he was so excited, and me trying to think who I'd call if we got arrested. We got to the entrance, and

I paid the admission. The girl took my money and didn't say anything. We went through the turnstile, and I started to think; maybe Junior was right. Fourth of July. Everybody welcome. Well that boy took off running right over to this merry-go-round of little cars and plopped himself down in the red one. He started jerking the little steering wheel back and forth and smiled up at me. 'Look Mamma, I'm drivin'!' But he never got to go 'round. I looked and saw some other little children pulling to get into the kiddie-cars, but their parents, seeing the dark child in the red car, held them back. Then I heard someone shout at me. 'Hey you!' I turned and saw this white fella grinning at me. 'What's the matter with you gal?' he said; This ain't no Juneteenth!' He gave me my money back. Take that kid and go, before you run off all my business.' Junior sat very still in that little car watching us. I went over and pulled him out of the car; he said 'We not gonna ride today, Mamma?' 'No, baby,' I said, 'not today. We'll come back another time.'

We sat at that bus stop for what seemed like years, watching the little white children come and go with their folks, laughing and carrying balloons and cotton-candy like they didn't have a care in the world. The bus finally got there just as the fireworks began to light up the sky. He looked out the bus window at them till we turned the corner and we couldn't see them anymore. Junior looked at me, real serious like and said; 'Don't cry Mamma'; do you remember? 'Don't cry. We gonna drive one day. One day we gonna drive, for real.'

(JR. and CLARICE embrace, as lights go to OUT.)

THE END

Gertrude Baker (top) and Kim Corbin in *Black Lily and White Lily*.
Photo by Roberta Barnes.

Black Lily
and White Lily

Note As You Read *Black Lily and White Lily*

With *Black Lily and White Lily,* Houston returns to the fifties milieu in San Antonio, TX. Through two perspectives, one black and one white, he re-creates dual lives, highlighting contrasting day-to-day realities and ambitions. Lily Winslow, the white nouveau rich lady of leisure, just wants to get through the day. She says, "I find sitting still to be the most underrated of activities." Lily Mae, her servant of twenty-seven years, wants a life of accomplishment beyond maid service. Speaking of her dream of owning a bus service, Lily Mae says, "I know how to work it; I know it would work! Hire me a good experienced road driver, and I'd handle the bookings, and the books." The interdependence of the two women, despite the race and economic divide, is a familiar theme in African American drama, e.g. Douglas Turner Ward's *A Day of Absence* (1965) and *Happy Ending (1965).*

The drama unfolds in a realistic/naturalistic style; in one scene the two watch television together and Lily Mae snaps green beans. A prologue introduces their relationship a few years before the main conflict of the story. It is followed by five scenes that alternate between monologues to the audience and dialogue between the two Lilys. They seem alone in a guilded cage of love and hate, respect and disrespect, and loyalty and betrayal.

Production Notes

Black Lily and White Lily was first presented on January 5, 1996 as part of the 14 Annual New Plays Festival at Cleveland Public Theatre, Cleveland Ohio with the following cast:

Sue Johnson	Lily Mae
Beverly Young Wykoff	Lily Winslow

Director: Nancy Burkinshaw

Black Lily and White Lily was revived as part of the "One Two Three" festival of one-act plays at the Guadalupe Cultural Arts Center and Palo Alto College in 2003, with Pamela Slocum and Antionette Winstead, directed by Ric Slocum.

Characters

Lily Mae   African American maid, middle-aged

Lily Winslow   White Southern Belle, in her 60s

Setting

Fashionable home in San Antonio, Texas, in the 1950s.

Prologue

(A pile of clothes spills out from an open suitcase. LILY M., a middle-aged African American woman, is putting on a dress over her head as lights up. Her employer, a white woman of similar age, watches.)

LILY W.: That's it. Now turn around. *(LILY M. moves)* No faster. Twirl around.

LILY M.: Twirl around? *(She spins until almost dizzy.)*

LILY W.: That's enough, now don't overdo it.

LILY M.: I really like this color, Mrs. Winslow. It brings out my skin tone.

LILY W.: Now, put on the jacket. Yes, and let it kind of fall off your shoulders, casual like. That's right. Now walk over there and turn around. *(LILY M. does action).*

LILY M.: Like this?

LILY W.: That's enough now. Take it off. I don't want to look at it any more. It reminds me of something. Something . . .

LILY M.: Something sad?

LILY W.: Why, no. Eh something wonderful . . .

LILY M.: Like what, if I may be so bold.

LILY W.: Lily Mae, you know that a real lady never reveals all her secrets. Not even to her dearest friend.

LILY M.: Am I your dearest friend?

LILY W.: Well, I don't know who is if you're not. Why else would I be giving you all these lovely things? Yes, that dress is better—turn, turn. I associate it with memories.

LILY M.: Didn't you wear this one to the Christmas Party at Seven Oaks?

LILY W.: Indeed I did, and what a deadly dull evening that was—all those Macallisters and Mavericks looking down their long brown noses at me. Old money can be so mean sometimes.

LILY M.: *(Puts on a flamboyant hat.)* Would you look at that, Miss Lily, sho nuff some hot stuff.

LILY W.: That would knock their eyes out at Sunday service.

LILY M. This might be a little too sassy for church, better after six to a chic cocktail affair . . .

LILY W.: Do you think I'm shallow?

LILY M.: What do you mean . . .

LILY W.: I mean, you know. Nothing. Well, I took this test in McCalls Magazine which revealed that, according to my low score I was quite a shallow person.

LILY M.: Don't pay no attention to that stuff. They just selling something you don't need is all.

LILY W.: Oh, you're right. You're right as usual. It must really bother you to be so right all the time. *(LILY M. concludes the dress up and stands in her slip as lights fade.)*

Scene 1

(A few years later)

(Lily Mae adjusts her hat looking into mirror. She wears a 1950s style tailored suit.)

LILY MAE: *(To audience)* Do you like the hat? It's a Lilly Daché, don't cha know. Just like the one Princess Grace Kelly wore on the cover of LIFE magazine. And this suit? Man tailored elegance from Lili-Anne of California. It's kinda funny that they share the same first name, Lily. That's the name of the lady that gave them to me, and it's my first name too. We're about the same size, except she's a little bigger in the bust. Shoot! That's no hill for a stepper. *(Takes falsies out of handbag and places them in suit.)* There. Miss Lily never likes to wear things more than two or three times. Good thing she married Eugene Winslow, The Motel King. Being a millionaire, he could afford her taste in shopping. Miz Lily Winslow was an all right woman to work for most of the time. She was born poor as Job's turkey so she did have her funny little ways after she married money. But she would give me little raises ever so often, and me and Rayetta lived decent. Rayetta's my grown daughter. I damn near never had to buy clothes, except for underwear and stockings of course. Gene Winslow used to like looking at me in Miz Winslow's old clothes. Said I looked better in them than she did. He sure could talk! Just full of bull corn. Or as the ladies say these days, bullshit, may he rest in peace. I was disappointed when he left me out of his will . . . after 27 years of service caring for his wives, his son, washing and ironing and such. Listen! I'll tell you something that's for real. You find out a lot about folks when you do their washing; what they had to eat, to drink, whether they sweat or bleed, if their bowels are loose or tight. *(Pause)* But I think I know why he did it. Left me out of his will, I mean. He didn't want Miz Lily to suspect anything . . . about us, him, and me. You know, that we would get, so to speak, real close every once in a while. It wasn't no big thing really; he never forced me; some do I know. But I knew what was what, and he did too. The next day I would find a hundred dollars in my shoe, or in the pocket of my apron. It came in handy with a child growing up and such and no man of my own to speak of. I never speak of Rayetta's daddy who used to run the road with the Brotherhood of Sleeping Car Porters. One day when she was about six, he just kept on running. Course, Rayetta would never wear Miz Lily's old clothes like I could. She always had to have new. Rayetta never liked Miz Lily much. Never did. She got so mad when I told her about me and Old Man Winslow. She said I wasn't nothing but a common whore. I thought she would understand; us being more like sisters than mother and daughter. Lord knows, you try to do what's right. I don't think she's ever respected me after that. Lord, children are such awful things. But where would we be without them, I guess.

Scene 2

(Lily Winslow, a lady of faded beauty, reclines on a chaise lounge and stares at the audience for a long count.)

LILY WINSLOW: *(To audience)* No. I haven't forgotten what I want to say. I find sitting still to be the most underrated of activities. And sitting still is quite a triumph for me personally. Not fidgeting, not talking, and most important of all, not smoking! It was my maid who got me to stop. She threatened me and insulted me and otherwise psychologically tortured me until I didn't have much choice. I quit. Cold turkey. None of that tapering-off nonsense. My maid was so grateful. The house didn't stink, and the sheer white curtains were actually white once more. So, I discovered that I am still capable of making someone a little happier even in my present state of dilapidation. That alone would have been reason enough to be off the things. I would never quit for health reasons. I know all about cancer. I am intimate with it. I spit in the face of cancer. Lung or throat or otherwise. My husband died of the stuff. Cigars. It started as a shiny little brown spot on his lower lip and spread rapidly, to his brain. It was awful. He even tried to light up a cigar in the oxygen tent. Even after his lip was removed. It wasn't pretty. I don't know what I would have done without Lily Mae's help and strength through it all. Lilly Mae's my maid. The only maid I've ever had. She was with my husband's family for years, practically raised his son Leo when Leo's mother died. Yes, I was his second wife. The second Mrs. Winslow. We met in Las Vegas about a hundred years ago. He was there at some real estate do, and I was working on the strip at the Sands as a showgirl, not a stripper as people love to think. Stripping takes talent, and I have absolutely none, except a talent for walking and smiling in a bathing suit and high heels with ten pounds of pink rooster feathers piled on top of my head. Boy, he was a sweet talker! I mean, the honey fairly dripped. We fell in love after a fashion; he with my face and body, and me with his motels. He owned five of them then. In Phoenix, Tucson, El Paso, San Antonio, and Corpus Christi. Well, doncha know, he took me on a tour of all of them. When we got to San Antonio, we got married, and he gave me one for a wedding present. The Alamo-Tel. I still own it too, though it quit making money years ago, when they built I-10 on top of it. I'm not a sentimental person as a rule, but when I am, I like to swim in sentiment. We honeymooned in Acapulco, at the Acapulco Princess. I still have the ashtray. When we came back to San Antonio, he moved me into this house, here on Contour Drive, where I have lived ever since. Lily Mae was already here when I arrived. We got along famously from the first. Oh, she wasn't called 'Lily Mae' back then. I had to add the 'Mae'. We couldn't very well both be called Lily now could we? Think of the confusion. I would call her Lily Mae, or just plain Mae in front of company. I don't think she liked it very much at first. But she got used to it over the years.

(Lights out)

Scene 3

(Lights up on the two women watching T.V. LILY W. is reclining holding remote control 'clicker'; LILY M. is seated in a chair, snapping green beans into a bowl.)

LILY W.: *(Clicks remote)* I hate Lucy in this period. This period when they went to Hollywood and every out-of-work actor in town made a guest appearance. Oh my God, Harpo Marx! Why do people find him funny? Do you think he's funny? I think it's rather sad, really. A poor mute with obviously deep, psychological problems. I can understand about Groucho. At least Groucho made funny cracks, but this one—dear Lord! Should I click him?

LILY M.: No ma'am. I like this part.

LILY W.: Do you think I'm lazy?

LILY M.: No Ma'am, I don't think you're lazy.

LILY W.: Like Pearl Bailey used to say, "I ain't lazy, I was just born tired."

LILY M.: That wasn't Pearl Bailey, that was . . .

LILY W.: Gene Winslow used to say I was the laziest white woman he ever saw.

LILY M.: What did he mean by that?

LILY W.: What are you snappin' those beans for Lily Mae? Don't we have frozen?

LILY M.: Probably so. I likes doing it. It's soothing. Snapping tender green beans. Just listen to that sweet little snap.

LILY W.: *(Reacting to T.V.)* Oh please! That does it. I'm clicking you Harpo.

LILY M.: Go head on click him if you want to. *(T.V. changes to all black rap video.)*

LILY W.: What in the world? Just look at those children! *(Pause)* What in heaven's name are you snapping snap beans for? Don't tell me you've taken up cooking at this late juncture.

LILY M.: Like I said. It soothes me. Anyhow, does it matter whether I've taken up cooking or not?

LILY W.: Well, of course it doesn't. I was just curious; there's no need to get so damn snappish about it. *(PHONE rings.)*

LILY M.: *(Answers phone.)* Winslow's residence. Oh, hello, hon. Unh huh. Unh huh. Not yet. No. I will! Unh huh. I know that, honey. Bye.

LILY W.: Was that Rayetta?

LILY M.: Unh huh. Yes.

LILY W.: Is everything all right?

LILY M.: Yes, fine; just fine. Mrs. Winslow. We need to have us a little talk.

LILY W.: Oh good! I like talking.

LILY M.: We have to turn off the television.

LILY W.: Why? I can listen and talk at the same time.

LILY M.: Fine. Suit yourself. Look. Look here, Mrs. Winslow; I'm quitting. I'm giving my two weeks notice now, and I . . .

LILY W.: You're what?

LILY M.: . . . And I want . . . I would like as my severance pay a check for five thousand dollars.

L.W: *(Shuts off T.V.)* You can't quit on me. What am I suppose to do for help for the rest of my life? You know how my knees swell up to the size of honeydew melons! I'm helpless!

LILY M.: Get yourself one of those strong young women from Mexico.

LILY W.: But I don't speak Mexican! You don't understand. What am I supposed to do? *(She wails.)*

LILY M.: For gosh sakes Mrs. Winslow, *Gone With The Wind* is over! *(LILY W. stops crying. Pause.)* It was a very long movie, but like all things, it eventually came to an end.

LILY W.: If I remember my Emily Post correctly, severance pay is only paid when the employer voluntarily terminates the employee, and not the other way around.

LILY M.: But after 27 years Mrs. Winslow, I . . .

LILY W.: If I were to accept the terms of your resignation, notice I did say "if," what in the world would you do with five thousand dollars?

LILY M.: Buy a bus.

LILY W.: A bus . . .

LILY M.: Yes ma'am; a bus.

LILY W.: What sort of bus?

LILY M.: A school bus.

LILY W.: A school bus.

LILY M.: That's right.

LILY W.: But why? Why in the world would you want to drive a school bus full of howling rug rats?

LILY M.: Not to drive it myself . . .

LILY W.: Well that's a relief, anyway.

LILY M.: You know how many churches there are around here? How many colored churches?

LILY W.: Quite a few I would imagine . . .

LILY M.: Yes ma'am, and they all have choirs; and they all go to other churches in other towns around here to sing and fellowship; and they all go to conventions and picnics and retreats and, well, you see what I mean? Why would they want to make Mr. Greyhound richer, when I can make them a better price?

LILY W.: I believe you are actually serious.

LILY M.: I know how to work it; I know it would work! I'd hire me a good experienced road driver, and I'd handle the bookings, and the books . . . and Rayetta would help of course . . .

LILY W.: Of course, Rayetta . . .

LILY M.: Well? What you say?

LILY W.: After all these years you could leave me and this house, at your age, to go driving up and down the highway and all hours with a bus load of singing sisters.

LILY M.: Sounds like heaven to me . . .

LILY W.: I just don't believe your nerve. After all I've done for you.

LILY M.: Here we go . . .

LILY W.: Given you the clothes off my back . . .

LILY M.: Which meant nothing to you.

LILY W.: Shared my home with you and my husband with you . . .

LILY M.: What do you mean by that remark, pray tell?

LILY W.: You know very well what I mean. Do you think I didn't know? Do you think he didn't tell me?

LILY M.: He told you?

LILY W.: I was his wife; of course he told me. Years ago. Do you think I care? I was glad to have him off me, even for one night.

LILY M.: He told you! My Lord! Don't you see? He disrespected both you and me, by telling you about it, that son of a bitch.

LILY W.: How very tragic. How very very southern Gothic tragedy!

LILY M.: *(Sobs and blows her nose into tissue.)*

LILY W.: For Pete's sake, what are you crying about? I'm the one should be crying. You expect me to pay you five thousand dollars for the privilege of leaving me high and dry after all these years, when you know I am practically an invalid; and you know how hard it is to break in good help in this day and age. Do you think I was born yesterday morning?

LILY M.: I'll help you find good help . . .

LILY W.: You just think about this for a minute. Think about somebody beside yourself for a minute. Without you I would have to let myself go completely to hell; I believe I would.

LILY M.: Mrs. Winslow, please . . .

LILY W.: Who else do I see, besides you? Who else do I see? Who? No one to be beautiful for . . . ever again. Never again . . . *(She sobs melodramatically.)*

LILY M.: That won't work Mrs. Winslow. That 'guilt' stuff.

LILY W.: And why not? It's been working for thousands of years.

LILY M.: Do you really think the slave chooses his chains?

LILY W.: I don't think anything. I don't think about it! *(Pause)* But, since you seem determined to go, I will write you a check for five thousand dollars.

LILY M.: Thank you, Jesus!

LILY W.: But I do so not as 'severance pay,' which is absurd, but as a little business loan, which you must pay back with interest.

LILY M.: *(Handing LILY W. her pocketbook.)* That's fine. I'll make the payments. Make it out in Rayetta's name.

LILY W.: *(Writing check.)* . . . And I do so for one reason and for one reason only which has nothing to do with me wanting to finance you in some 'I Love Lucy' scheme that is, no doubt, doomed to failure, as well as requiring me to deprive myself of your irreplaceable service.

LILY M.: Yes ma'am, I hate to do it but . . . What reason?

LILY W.: It will be worth the pleasure I will feel, when you come crawling back to me, and I will then be able to utter the most satisfying words in the English language. I. Told. You. So. *(Hands check to LILY M. She kisses it.)* *(Lights out)*

Scene 4

(LILY M. is dressed as in Scene 1; addresses audience.)

LILY M.: Suddenly, there I was: an entrepreneur! Business was real good that first summer. The National Baptist Convention was in Austin that year, and I took up three full loads in nine hours going and coming. I made a little over seven hundred dollars, after I'd paid my expenses. I stayed up there that whole week-end shuttling the folks from the hotel to the various churches in town; Ebenezer, Brown's Chapel, First Baptist, Second Baptist, Mt. Zion, Mt. Shiloh, Mt. Sinai, Mt. Calvery, Mt. Olive, and the rest. At each church, I passed out cards and drummed up more business. I was a natural born businesswoman, which seemed to surprise everyone but me. How'd they think I ran the Winslow's house all them years? By hook or crook? I opened up two or three charge accounts; put me a down payment on a new little Chevrolet, even paid old lady Winslow a few payments back, much to her surprise. Yes, I was living the American dream sure enough. And then the incident, as it came to be called, took place--out on Highway 10, just outside of Ft. Stockton, which was our rest stop between here and El Paso. We were coming back from the Eastern Star spring retreat, which was held in El Paso that year. Did I say that already? Rayetta says I tend to repeat myself like an old lady, but what can you expect, know what I mean? Anyway, the incident, as it happened was not the result of too much beer drinking and a weak bladder, as the gossip goes. Unh uh. It was just old Mr. Mulkey, in confusion, and the fact that he had lost his eyeglasses, had simply relieved himself against the big back tire of the bus. Because he couldn't find the colored restroom, which of course had gone out of business years before; and he refused to use what he thought was the white restroom, which just said 'Men' on the door. He got very agitated, as he explained it later, and his agitation put pressure on his bladder, so he couldn't' hold it, so, well, he just went on an urinated against the back tire. Poor thing. He was too near-sighted to see the mother and little daughter coming out of the Baskin-Robbins, or the Highway Patrolman just pulling in for a doughnut. He was just in time to see old Mr. Mulkey do his business, and hear the lady scream. He ran over and handcuffed Mr. Mulkey, and Mr. Mulkey started crying, thought they were gonna lynch him I expect. He tried to explain himself, but it was no use.

It was terrible. Just terrible. The mamma screamed again and ran over all red-faced telling the Highway Patrol that that old darkey had ruined her little daughter for life. Talking 'bout he shook his penis in her little pink face. He was just shaking off the last little drips, you know, the way men do so they don't stain their underwear. But God above knows, people see what they want to see; or what they NEED to see, which is even worse. Somehow it got into the newspapers down here; the Express News gave it a headline like it was World War III. "Local Flasher Terrorizes Ft. Stockton," or some such thing. Well. That was the end of my touring bus business. I had to pay Mr. Mulkey's bail, then his legal fees and fine. The judge thought one thousand dollars and ten years probation was about fair for such a terrible crime. On top of that, I got sued by Baskin Robbins people. Said their business was ruined when the story got around. Shoot; THEIR business. My insurance was cancelled. You can't transport people without insurance, you know. That was that. I sold the bus. What else could I do? I took a little loss on it all, I admit that, but I still had my health, right? Anything is possible if you got your health.

(Lights go down)

Scene 5

(Lights up on LILY W. She is as before, but now, a bit disheveled, news-papers, pop-bottles and assorted trash are about her on the floor. After a pause she speaks.)

LILY W.:   I had a rather disturbing meditation this afternoon. Sometimes when I'm sitting, just holding still, like I like to do, the stillness produces phenomena out of itself--sometimes monsters, sometimes angels, sometimes a clear white light. This afternoon, a face came to me out of the stillness, just as clear as anything . . . my mother's face. My old mother looking for all the world like she did the day she dropped dead after not being sick a day in her life. Stroke, they said. Massive. Went like THAT. She was an elementary school teacher in Louisiana, poor thing and she dropped dead in September of 1955--the year that Brown vs. Board of Education took effect. My dear mother, for some reason, just hated the colored. Just hated them. Like ice. It didn't matter to her how nice any of them were, or clean and polite. Brown vs. Board of Education was the Supreme Court decision that integrated the public schools in the South, starting with the first grade. My dear mother had taught first grade for over forty years. Some said she died of a broken heart. She used to tell me when I was a little girl; 'Now Lillian, you just cannot let your inferior races get any idea that there as good as us. Once you open that door, even a crack, there'd be no turning back. It's like wiping your behind on a wagon wheel; there's just no end to it.' In the middle of my meditation this afternoon, my mother's face smiled at me, like she was just right above my head looking down. Mother never smiled, but sure enough, there she was, just smiling away. She was holding a little bible which she opened to a verse I had never heard before. It read: beware ye the underdog, for he givith a deadly bite. *(PHONE rings. She answers it.)* Hello? Oh, hello stranger? Has the Baptist church made you a millionaire yet? What? Why yes, of course you can come over. I would love to talk to you as always. Bye. *(She hangs up and tidies-up as best she can without leaving the chaise. After a moment, LILY MAE appears at her doorway, carrying a small suitcase.)*

LILY M.: I'm back.

LILY W.: So I see. Come in, come in; we're not strangers, are we? *(LILY M. takes a few steps in.)* My knees have gone down quite a bit, since the last time you were here. Did you notice?

LILY M.: They look about the same to me, Mrs. Winslow.

LILY W.: Well they're not. They've gone down quite a bit. I didn't imagine it.

LILY M.: No ma'am, I guess you didn't. How's the new woman doing?

LILY W.: What new woman? Oh, her. I had to fire her. Weeks ago. A thief I can stand, but a liar, never! I've managed quite all right by myself. I think.

LILY M.: Yes, I can see that you have.

LILY W.: *(Pause)* Well . . . ?

LILY M.: Well . . . Mrs. Winslow, I would like my old position back if . . .

LILY W.: I don't mean that, silly! Well, didn't you miss me?

LILY M.: I suppose I did, miss you, in a manner of speaking.

LILY W.: I knew you would. And I missed you too, Lily Mae. Well course you can have your old job back.

LILY M.: Ain't you going to say it?

LILY W.: Say what?

LILY M.: You know. The most powerful words in the English language . . .

LILY W.: No. No, I'm not. Now that you're really here, I take no pleasure in humiliating you. I'm just glad to see you. And to know that things turned out all right. I feel sorry for you. I actually do. Come on in and rest your handbag. *(LILY M. does so.)* Turn on the television *(She does.)* And give me a little neck rub will you please. *(She begins massage.)* Nobody has hands like yours . . .

LILY M.: I still intend to pay you back all you loaned me. With interest, but it'll have to be a little at a time, but you know I'm good for it, even if it takes . . . *(LILY W. bursts out laughing.)*

LILY W.: Oh, Lily Mae, Lily Mae! I guess I can tell you now. Ha Ha! Life is really so funny. Know, what I mean, so flat out funny!

LILY M.: Tell me what? What's funny?

LILY W.: You don't have to pay me back at all. Not one nickel, not one penny . . . !

LILY M.: Don't play with my nerves, now. Tell me what you mean.

LILY W.: I mean it was your money all along. Isn't that great?

LILY M.: What do you mean, 'mine'?

LILY W.: I mean yours, silly Mae. Gene Winslow left it to you in his will, five thousand dollars, exactly. I was his executrix, of course, and I just never bothered to tell you about it; just kept it between me and my attorneys. I figured I'd give it to you some day, if you were a good girl. And I did give it to you. I actually did. Isn't life funny?

LILY M.: Why? Why?

LILY W.: As I remember, I was a little p.o.'ed at you, right after the old man died. You going around acting more like the widow than me. I grieved too. I just grieved in my own way. I intended to give it to you someday. And after a while, it slipped my mind. And then you asked me for it. Ha! Isn't it funny the way life turns out? *(Massage continues.)*

LILY M.: Do you know how easy it would be to kill you, right now? . . . to take your windpipe between my thumbs, and just snap?

(Lights start down)

LILY W.: Stop. Stop it! Now! *(Lights out)* You're tickling me, Lily Mae! Lily M. . . . !!!

THE END

La Frontera

a play with music

Note As You Read *La Frontera*

La Frontera is a one-act play in 5 scenes about borders; in this case, cultural borders that often undermine understanding and trust. Many moments in the work reflect traditional realistic dramaturgy in the development of the story of a Mexican family moving into a traditionally African American neighborhood. However, the work parts from traditional realism with intermittent musical numbers that offer commentary on serious and light hearted issues, e.g., the play begins and ends with a song. Houston highlights the similarities between ethnic cultures who consider themselves different.

The characters express the central motif of the work early in the play in the following dialogue between mother and daughter:

> DORIS: Birds of a Feather are always happier together. That's what Big Mama used to say. I've got nothing against the races mixing, as long as they're decent clean, and . . .

> SONIA: . . . like us. We could put a big mirror in the driveway and live in a perfect parallel world.

This exchange is an interesting ironic element in this drama that uses parallelism in characters, actions, and concerns to throw into relief the common human concerns of the Hispanic/Latino family and the African American family. The families are mirror images of each other throughout the play. Visually you see both households at the same time, and often they speak the same lines simultaneously, though in their different households. Both families have three generations represented— a grandmother, a middle aged couple, and a teenager daughter. They express similar suspicion about each other because of perceived differences, and both families reflect on the need for economic security and the desire for a safe environment for their children at home and school.

It is a light comic drama with an upbeat message that people can live together if they believe they can and try. It is in the tradition of Ossie Davis' *Purlie Victorious,* a play mocking old stereotypes and prejudice that shows blacks and whites, especially the younger generation, bridging and crossing borders and working together.

Production Notes

La Frontera was first produced in 1993 at the Guadalupe Cultural Arts Center in San Antonio by JumpStart Performance Co. in collaboration with the Guadalupe on a double bill that included *Las Nuevas Tamaleras* by Alicia Mena. Houston's work was commissioned by the Mid-America Arts Alliance. It was produced with the following cast:

Lola Ybarra	Veronica Gonzales
Hector Ybarra	Roger Alvarez
Rosalinda	Lisa Suarez
Carl Wilson	George Staly
Doris Wilson	Kitty Williams
Sonia Wilson	Alisa Claridy
Buelita	Lisa Suarez
Big Mama	Alisa Claridy

Music by Tito Villalobus Moreno
Directed by Max Parilla

Characters

Lola Ybarra	Mother, 30-ish
Hector Ybarra	Father, 30-ish
Rosalinda Ybarra	Daughter, 16
Carl Wilson	Father
Doris Wilson	Mother
Sonia Wilson	Daughter, 17
Buelita	Grandmother Ybarra
Big Mama	Grandmother Wilson

Setting

The present. Two adjacent houses on the East Side of San Antonio, Texas, near downtown.

Scene 1

(Partial view of two houses, with driveway, yard between; house SL is overgrown with weeds and has a 'for sale' sign in front. In background is a view of the Tower of the Americas and the towers of the Alamodome.)

(Song sung by COMPANY offstage)

> Between day and night
> Falls the border
> Of dawn's early light-
> Between left and right
> Slips the shadow that nobody likes—
>
> The ocean and the sand;
> The river and the land;
> Between you and me
> There's a mountain that's too big to see

(HECTOR YBARRA removes sign from yard.)

> La la la, la la la; La Frontera!
> Running like a borderline straight through my heart
> La la la, la la la; La Fronteee-ra!
> Running like a borderline,
> To keep us apart . . . !

(Lights up on SONIA doing homework and listening to a Walkman. After a moment she sees that DORIS has entered.)

SONIA: Hi Mom. What's up with that long face?

DORIS: Hi Sugar. Daddy's not home yet? How's school?

SONIA: Don't want to talk about it? I understand Mom. You're probably suffering from Black-woman's Burnout. The combined stresses of job, family, and being black and female in America can create chronic clinical depression. I saw it on Montel Williams, so you know it's true.

DORIS: Work is O.K It's this neighborhood. Somebody torched another house on Hackberry. That's four in one block. It's sad to see this old neighborhood go away before my eyes.

SONIA: I know. And if I see another pregnant 13 year old girl
. . . don't worry Mom; I don't intend to make you a grandmamma till
you're old and gray.

DORIS: . . . And you're old and married. I noticed the 'For Sale' sign
is gone from next door?

SONIA: Guess that means we'll be getting new neighbors.

DORIS: Yeah, I hope they're . . . you know . . . like us.

SONIA: Like us? You mean a nuclear age family?

DORIS: I mean . . . of Color.

SONIA: Well, I don't think the East Side has to worry about an inva-
sion from Alamo Heights . . .

DORIS: Birds of a Feather are always happier together. That's what
Big Mama used to say. I've got nothing against the races mixing, as
long as they're decent clean, and . . .

SONIA: . . . like us. We could put a big mirror in the driveway and
live in a perfect parallel world.

DORIS: Not a bad idea. But you know me; I'm a child of the sixties. You know; make love not war; not a prejudiced bone in my
body . . . the girls at the shop where I work are sweet as can be. I have
no problem with Chicanos . . .

SONIA: Mom; you can't call Mexicans "Chicanos" anymore that's
like calling yourself a soul sister.

DORIS: What now; these things change so fast . . . I remember when
being called a colored person seemed like an improvement. But my
mother . . . I don't know what it was, but she did not like Chi . . . what
should I say now?

SONIA: Hispanics.

DORIS: Hispanics. Of course. But your grandmother neither
liked nor trusted any of them. Lord knows why, cause she was part
Comanche herself, and proud of it.

SONIA: I hope I live long enough to see the day when race doesn't
have to be topic "A."

DORIS: Hear her prayer, lord! What are you working on?

SONIA: It's my history homework. I'm writing about African explorers before the diaspora. Very interesting. I'm thinking of changing my major.

DORIS: Really? But you've always wanted to be an architect, since before you could even pronounce it. *(CARL enters.)* Hi. Carl, you're just in time to hear your daughter is changing her major.

SONIA: I was kidding.

CARL: Good. We'll need architects to rebuild this neighborhood, and soon at the rate it's going. It's this damn recession. I see they torched another house down the street. I know things are supposed to be getting better, but it hasn't trickled down to where we live.

(Sings) I work at city hall.
> I'm a clerk at city hall.
> In the records department
> Lower level.
> It's a good job
> With a retirement pension!
> Recessionary Blues.

DORIS: I know just what you mean honey.
(Sings)
> Cause I work at North Star Mall
> I'm a clerk at North Star Mall
> In the floral department
> of Marshall Fields.
> It's a good job
> And I was lucky to get it!
> Recessionary Blues.

SONIA: *(Sings)*
> It's my senior year at Highlands High
> So I persevere at Highlands High
> Cause it won't be long now
> Til graduation-
> I'll need a real good job—
> Paying tuition!
> Recessionary Blues.

ALL: *(Sing)*
>My self-image to survive
>Doesn't need
>A Mercedes to drive—
>My paid-for Chevrolet will
>Get me through the roughest day—
>I'm caught up with my bills
>Your love still gives me chills,
>And I'm here to say
>It's mine all mine.

CARL: (Sings)
>Which is more than I can say for this house
>We got a loan with Bank of the South
>And we'll pay off the interest by
>The turn of the century—
>But it's a nice house
>And we were lucky to get it!
>Recessionary Blues!

DORIS: You notice the sign was gone from next door. Wonder who our new neighbors will be?

CARL: Wonder no more, my girl. The deed happened across my desk on the way to escrow. Our new neighbors are a family named Ybarra!

Scene 2

A Home of Our Own

(Crossfade to YBARRA house as ROSALINDA, HECTOR and LOLA enter singing.)

LOLA: Look HECTOR, Look! There's a view of the tower!

ROSALINDA: Look Papi, Look! My own bathroom with shower and a room of my own, with my own private phone!

HECTOR: Si, porsupuesto, but don't think you are grown; you're only a sophomore.

LOLA: Only a sophomore ...

ROSALINDA: Only a sophomore, but with her own private phone.

LOLA: Look Hector, Look! There's room for a garden--tomatoes, and corn, and calavacita. This dirt is so black!

HECTOR: *(sotto voce)* Just like the neighborhood.

LOLA: Dirt is so rich!

ROSALINDA: *(sotto voce)* Not like the neighborhood!

ALL: I think we've come home—to a home of our own!!

HECTOR: *(Spoken)* This neighborhood is in what they call a blighted area. That means the banks will be glad to give yon a low interest loan, just to get you to live here. *(They sign papers.)*

LOLA: El Senor he works in mysterious ways ...

ROSALINDA: He got a promotion along with a raise!

HECTOR: That's right! Shake hands with the city's newest Sanitation Department field supervisor!

LOLA: So we can make payments; it's heaven sent.

HECTOR: We can make payments, low interest payments ...

ALL: It's practically cheaper than rent!

(They move into house; ROSALINDA is last; she lingers a moment before going in.)

ROSALINDA: Home at last!

Scene 3

(LOLA and ROSALINDA are working in the yard planting, weeding, etc. BIG MAMA enters and stares at them or a long moment, after which LOLA sees her.)

LOLA: Oh! Hello, how are you?

ROSALINDA: Hi.

BIG MAMA: How do?

LOLA: *(After a stiff pause.)* Gotta stay ahead of these weeds around here, or they'll just take over.

BIG MAMA: I know that's the truth. *(She goes into WILSON house as lights change. DORIS is making a flower arrangement.)* Anybody home?

DORIS: Hi, Big Mama.

BIG MAMA: Hi. What's going on out there?

DORIS: What do you mean?

BIG MAMA: I mean, I hope to heaven those girls I just saw are just doing yardwork for whoever bought that house and not . . .

DORIS: Those are our new neighbors. The Ybarras. They seem nice.

BIG MAMA: Nice? You're gonna need burglar bars on each and every one of these windows.

DORIS: Stop it. You haven't even met them yet.

BIG MAMA: I don't want to meet them. Everybody knows they all belong to gangs, even the old ones.

DORIS: Where did you get that . . . ?

BIG MAMA: Everybody knows it but you, and you better get hip to the program!

DORIS: Mama, have you been watching cable TV again? You know it just gets you all upset. Please stick to your soap operas.

BIG MAMA: I don't watch those things, too much sex. I know I'm an old woman now; nobody listens to me anymore. But it's a known fact that people who take their mother's advice live longer. All I'm telling you is "watch out"; and for land's sake, don't turn your back. Where's Sonia Diane? Where's my grandbaby? Come give Big Mama some sugar, honey . . . *(She exits.)*

DORIS: *(To audience)* I'd like to tell you something about my mother. She won't tell you herself, but you need to know. She's not a mean person. I learned kindness from her. But when she talks sometimes, you can't help but notice that she's afflicted with prejudice. A pre-judgment of fellow human beings, based not on them as individual creatures of the one creator, but on some single fact, some incident, some story from somewhere in the hurtful past. With each telling and re-telling of that story it gains momentum, until it posseses the authority of legend. And saddest of all, some part of that story found its way into my heart, in spite of my efforts to rub it away. *(Lights. music under.)*

Scene 4

(SONIA and ROSALINDA enter from opposite sides, carrying school books etc. ROSALINDA is wearing a Catholic school uniform, and SONIA is listening to a Walkman.)

ROSALINDA: Hi. Hello?

SONIA: Hi. What's going on?

ROSALINDA: Oh, not much. You know . . .

SONIA: Yeah. How do you like your new neighborhood? Is everything O.K.?

ROSALINDA: Yes, it's fine. People aren't too friendly though, I notice. We've been here three months, and you and your mom are the only ones who even speak to us.

SONIA: Don't worry about that. I've lived here all my life and some of them don't speak to me either. Look at those books. You must have a lot of homework!

ROSALINDA: All for one class, too. Cultural Anthropology.

SONIA: That sounds hard.

ROSALINDA: It's pretty interesting, about how we all got to be who we are. If I understand it right, everybody is a big mixture of many ancient tribes. So we might really be cousins if we go back far enough.

SONIA: I'm not too big on the social sciences. I'm going to be an architect, you know.

ROSALINDA: Why?

SONIA: So I can be a part of something big, something built to last—a church building, a bridge, a home for a family. To know that I had a hand in it . . . !

ROSALINDA: I'd be happy if I could be a good wife and mother. But economic realities being what they are, I'd better go for my MBA.

SONIA: You're right about that, girlfriend. But you may not get married for a long time . . .

ROSALINDA: The women in my family land too many young. It's a cultural thing. I've already got him picked out. *(She shows photo from wallet.)* Angel!

SONIA: Just be sure you use some sort of protection; this is the '90s. Not a good time to take chances.

ROSALINDA: Protection? Oh, you mean rubbers. I'm not worried about it. I intend to wait until my wedding night . . .

SONIA: And what about Angel? Will he wait too? You know how boys lie.

ROSALINDA: He better wait, if he knows what's good for him.

SONIA: If you know what's good for you, you'd better use . . .

ROSALINDA: . . . Self-control; not birth-control.

SONIA: That's all well and good, but let me drop the 911 on you . . .

(Song beat begins for "No Love without the Glove")

(Rap)
    If you go out with "Joe"
    You always know what might be
    On that bad-boy's mind;
    If he looks at you twice,
    You might think: "That's nice!"
    The next thing; you are the foolish kind.
    With a slip of the tongue,
    May let all come undone.

And things could easily get out of hand;
So don't get drastic
Without the plastic,
If you want to live to love again,
Remember—

BOTH:

No love without the glove,
No affection without protection.
No love without the glove-
Do it for your own protection—

ROSALINDA:

Sex-relations
Can cause complications;
So I don't let myself get carried away;
Cause when it comes to passion
I'm old fashioned;
I'm gonna wait until my wedding day.
If I choose to abstain
A virgin to remain
Until he walks me down the aisle
I'll remember your song
That day, and I'll stand up strong
And tell my husband with a radiant smile.
(I'll tell him-)

No love without the glove,
No affection without protection.
No love without the glove
Do it for your own protection.

(Repeat chorus)

(At end of song HECTOR comes out of house, and CARL comes from around front; they watch girls for a moment, and HECTOR pulls ROSALINDA away, then CARL does same with SONIA.)

HECTOR: Come on home Rosalinda, I'm sure Sonia has to go do her homework. Right, Mr. Wilson? That's right Mr. Ybarra. You doing O.K.?

HECTOR: Really good. Yourself?

CARL: Fine. Okey dokey. Yeah, well . . .

HECTOR: How 'bout those Spurs, eh?

CARL: Yeah, ain't they something.

HECTOR: Yeah, well; see you later.

CARL: Right. Later.

(They usher girls to opposite sides.)

HECTOR: What the hell was that about? Was I hearing you right? A rap song about . . . *(Gulps)* . . . about . . .

ROSALINDA: Contraception.

HECTOR: Don't talk dirty to me. I'm your father.

ROSALINDA: There's nothing dirty about it.

HECTOR: What kind of ideas is that Sonia putting in your head?

ROSALINDA: A rap song never got anybody pregnant, Popi.

HECTOR: I think you better go to your room and think about how you've been behaving lately.

ROSALINDA: De veras? Go to my very own room. O.K. *(Exits)*

CARL: I told you about performing in the street, young lady, wasting your talent on folks that don't appreciate it!

SON IA: Daddy, I was trying to maybe save her life!

CARL: What about your life? We didn't bring you up to be running around the streets with just any old body.

(SONIA exits as DORIS and LOLA enter each going to her husband. A parallel scene unfolds in which the wives and then the husbands speak in unison intermittently as both couples reflect on the past.)

DORIS & LOLA: What's the matter?

CARL: Your daughter's been carrying on in the street like some wild woman.

HECTOR: Tu hija se estaba portando como una mujer de la calle!

LOLA: Oh, young girls sometimes have more energy than they know what to do with.

DORIS: It's a hormonal thing!

CARL: What's gotten in to you?

HECTOR: Whose side are you on?

DORIS & LOLA: I remember when you didn't mind harmones so much—

HECTOR: Bill, that was different . . .

CARL: We were more mature at their age.

DORIS: We were married at eighteen.

HECTOR: We knew what we were doing. My mother thought she wanted to kill you, till she got to know you. Then she was sure.

HECTOR & CARL: I'll never forget our first date . . .

HECTOR: I drove my Dad's old 1958 Lord Fairlane up to the limestone cliffs above Sunken Garden and pulled over along the road near the top to a spot known as Inspiration Point. You and your novia could look up at the moon and stars and look down on whatever was on the stage below, and beyond to the spreading lights of the city. It was my senior year at old Brackenridge High, and my future spread out before me like those city lights. I felt like the king of the world, because sitting next to me on the front seat was the prettiest sweetest girl in the whole school. I almost had a heart attack as she reached out and took my hand . . .

LOLA: I was a transfer student from Sidney Lanier; it's hard to change schools anytime, but in your senior year when you have to leave all your old friends, and try to make new ones among people who have known each other for years . . . But Hector was so sweet to me. He made me feel like I really belonged. Some of the girls thought I shouldn't go out with him; said he was too short for me. But I knew he was tall inside . . .

CARL: When me and Doris met, I knew from the first time I looked at her that she would be mine forever. I knew, cause it was one of those nights.

DORIS: What do you mean, Carl?

CARL: One of those San Antonio nights that only happen in the early spring, when the honeysuckle fills the air with a perfume so sweet and thick that it would shame an Arabian garden. One of those lingering barbecue smelling, winter banishing, lightning-bug bespangled evenings, when a young man's thoughts turn naturally to things tender and of the flesh . . .

DORIS: Speak on, baby.

CARL: My cousin Ray was in town from Houston to get together with this chick he'd met up there, see, who was visiting her aunt, and she had given him her number. He called, and we went over. She lived over on Potomac Street across the street from the graveyard. Turned out Ray's girl had a cousin too, and this cousin, Maxine, had a roommate at Prairie View A&M, who came in with her to go to the last game of the season, and on that hot spring night in 1966, we went for a walk through the graveyard, and somehow her hand found mine.

DORIS: I was never afraid of dead folks. Just living ones . . .

CARL: Not a dog barked, not a cricket cricked as we stared into each others eyes under a lull moon which shone like a pale blue light bulb in our basement of love!

DORIS: Carl, you're a poet.

CARL: In my heart's ear, I can still hear the sweet music that got us dancing oh so close that magical night. A song so pure and clear, it cut through all my doubts and teenage fear about who I was and if I was man enough for such a fine woman.

(Song begins at YBARRA house and continues with ensemble.)

Tu Y Yo

LOLA: Las canciones son mi vida—

DORIS: I hear my life in every song—

ALL: In the still of the night,
      Volver volver!

CARL: One summer night
       when we were young

HECTOR. & LOLA: Yo te quiero por mi alma

DORIS: I fell in love with all my soul.

ALL: When that deep purple falls
      Sabor a Mi!

HECTOR: Oldies but goodies turned gold.

ALL: Tu Y Yo!
      I'll love you longer than the rivers flow-
      Till there're no heros at the Alamo
      Tu Y Yo!

LOLA: Las canciones son me vida! etc.

(Repeat till 'Tu Y Yo' chorus.)

(At last part of song, BUELITA enters with a chair and sits, knitting. When music ends, LOLA, HECTOR, CARL, and DORIS exit.)

BUELITA: ¡Ahora, sigo yo para hablar . . . ! Y voy a hablar aunque no les guste lo que voy a decir. ¡Los Negros no son igual que nosotros . . . y esa es la realidad—hecho y derecho! Yo se que DE ESO no pueden hacer nada, pero a mi no me importa. I don' care. Yo ya estoy vieja y los viejos no tienen alternaliva—solo decir la verdad. El acercamiento de la muerte nos quita toda necesidad de ser amable . . . Y apestan! Como huevo y tocino. La unica manera de vivir entre esa gente, es hacer unas cercas grandotas y fuertes; y hablar puro Espanol. Y claro, se necesitan unas rejas para la ventana, ¿Como se yama? Los bur-gler bars, si vamos evitar robos. Y todos ellos son de bandillas; hasta los padres. ¡Ay, yo solo le pido a mi Diosito que me guarde unos cuantos afios mas, para poder protejer a mi preciosa nietecita de las manos cochinas de esos negritos locos que siempre andan en la calle como una bola de perros buscando una virgen inocente para raptar!

LOLA: Who are you talking to, Mama?

BUELITA: The only person worth talking to anymore. Myself.

LOLA: It's good to see you. You don't come visit much lately.

BUELITA: Well now that you have moved to this foreign land, it's not so easy, you know. It's a long bus ride from Lombrano Street.

LOLA: You know Hector or I will be glad to pick you up, if you just call . . .

BUELITA: I don't want you to go to any trouble on my account . . .

LOLA: It's no trouble . . .

BUELITA: Where's Rosalinda? Donde esta mi preciosa? Rosalinda! Rosalinda! Your old 'Buelita is calling you!

LOLA: She'll be back soon. She went over to McCreless Mall with the girl from next door. You know how young girls are . . .

BUELITA: And I know how young boys are, too. You didn't let her run off with one of those . . .

LOLA: Our neighbors are nice hard working tax paying citizens like us. I'm sure she's fine . . .

(HECTOR enters.)

HECTOR: Hi!

BUELITA: Hector, please take me over to McCreless Mall right away! I need to buy a few things . . . Hurry up, I'll be wailing in the car . . . *(She goes.)*

HECTOR: What's with her?

LOLA: She's having one of her little spells. Do you mind taking her? She won't calm down until she sees Rosalinda.

HECTOR: Be seeing you . . .

LOLA: Thanks, you are a sweetheart. *(They kiss and HECTOR goes.)* I've always had the feeling that my mother would have been happier living in the 19th century. And here we are on the edge of the 21st, still worried about who's got the deepest tan. There's a story she tells of my grandmother's courtship long ago. She told me . . .

PROMENADE *(Song)*
>When her mother was the age of my child
>They lived in Mexico City,
>Across the street from Chapultepec Park,
>The most romantic place in Mexico City,
>After dark, After dark—
>
>When a nice young girl blossoms into young womanhood.
>She would go with her mother in the afternoon,
>To the Zocolo, or Chapultepec Park,
>And her mother would sit with all the other mothers.
>As the young girls strolled in a clock-wise direction,
>Around the fountain and the beautiful gardens,
>Hiding their eyes from the pretty young boys
>Walking counterclockwise glancing over their shoulders
>At the pretty young girls
>As they promenade . . .
>Properly promenade . . .
>
>One late afternoon in early September,
>She caught the eye of a guy with a front tooth of gold,
>She told her mother, and her mother told his mother,
>And they all made sure that the young man was told.
>He was handsome and strong, from a very good family;
>That was my grandfather, Encarnacion.

(Spoken)
And very well named was my grandfather, for he was surely the living
incarnation of my grandmother's hopes and dreams.

(Song continues)
>He was the son of the secretary
>To a cabinet minister of President Maderos,
>And though he was bright with a promising future,
>Came the revolution, and they all had to go.
>So they moved themselves to San Antonio,
>It was hard to start over, but after a while,
>They bought a little house by Mission San Juan,
>Grandfather, Grandmother, and my mother, their child.
>But that very next year, he died of consumption.
>So she went to work cleaning house all day long

For a family, who lived in a beautiful mansion,
But she dreamed of her husband in heaven as he was
At the Promenade, in her dreams he would properly
Promenade . . .

(At the end of song, ROSALINDA rushes on and runs to the front of her house. She is followed by HECTOR, SONIA and BUELITA.)

BUELITA: It's a good thing we went over there. She was just about to get into some big time trouble!

LOLA: What happened, Hector?

HECTOR: Not much. They were just walking around. Drinking cokes and talking. Some boys from Sonia's school were talking to them that's all, and listening to that rap music.

BUELITA: That's all? Drinking cokes! Everybody knows that leads to the hard stuff! And the next thing you know, she's pregnant or in jail. You know how they are . . . !

CARL: *(He and DORIS come out of their house.)* What's the problem. Are you alright, Sonia?

SONIA: I'm fine, dad. Just a little misunderstanding . . .

LOLA: The girls were talking to some boyfriends down at McCreless and . . .

SONIA: They weren't boyfriends. Just guys I go to school with . . .

CARL: I thought you were going to the library, young lady.

BUELITA: ¡Los Negros son malos, y solamenle piensan en sexo!

DORIS: What was that? What did that old lady say about 'negroes'?

HECTOR: Don't call her that old lady! That's my mother-in-law you're talking to.

CARL: Don't you raise your voice at my wife.

LOLA: He didn't mean anything. Let's calm down. Maybe we never should have moved over here. If we aren't willing to at least listen to each other . . . !

HECTOR: Or maybe they should move, if they don't like the way things are changing around here.

CARL: My mortgage is damn near paid off. I'll be damned if we're moving anywhere! Maybe you should move back to the Westside!

BUELITA: ¿Que tienen el Wes'side? ¡A mi me gusta el Wes'side!

HECTOR: And who's gonna make me? You?

CARL: What do you mean? You . . . !

SON IA: Stop it please!

(Lights dim)

Scene 5

(A few days later. Doris enters carrying a flowering plant, crosses to the YBARRA house and knocks.)

HECTOR: *(Off)* Just a second. *(He enters)* Oh, hello . . .

DORIS: How's it going? I though your wife might like these. They're Easter Lilies. We just got them in the store today.

HECTOR: That's nice of you, thanks. Lola's out right now, but she'll love them . . .

DORIS: Then I'll come back later . . .

HECTOR: Don't rush off, she'll be right back. Why don't you come in for a minute?

BOTH: I'm really sorry about the other day.

HECTOR: Rosalinda makes me a little crazy, but that wasn't necessary . . .

DORIS: We're the ones who should apologize . . .

(CARL enters and goes into his house.)

HECTOR: I guess there's enough blame to go around.

DORIS: Right. No need to fight over it. *(Both laugh)*

DORIS: We weren't being the best role models for our kids, now, were we?

HECTOR: Someday I hope to be as smart as my daughter. Coffee?

(Lights cross fade to WILSON house. LOLA enters carrying a package and knocks on door.)

LOLA: Hi. Anybody home?

CARL: Hey. What's going on.

LOLA: Is Doris home?

CARL: She should be any minute now. Come on in.

LOLA: The ladies at St. Leo's, that's my church, made tamales today, and I brought you a couple of dozen.

CARL: Thanks.

LOLA: Do you like tamales?

CARL: Is the pope catholic?

LOLA: He is at St. Leo's. About the other day . . .

CARL: I feel bad about that. I know we can do better.

(Crossfade)

DORIS: *(Taking coffee from HECTOR)* Thanks. Your house looks so nice. You know, I'm really glad you and Lola bought this house, in spite of the other day. The only hope the poor old East Side has is families like us.

HECTOR: Right. We got to make it nice for our kids, nice enough for them to want to stay and raise their kids here. Or else it'll all get swallowed up by dome parking lots . . .

DORIS: I know that's right. We need to start a neighborhood association! So we can look out for each other like they do in Monte Vista!

HECTOR: Yeah. Put up a united front when we have to fight!

(Crossfade)

CARL: Here's my business card; I wrote our home phone number on the back so you can call and let us know if you see anything going one that doesn't look right.

LOLA: You know I will; I'm one nosey woman.

CARL: Give me yours too.

(Crossfade)

DORIS: This neighborhood is changing fast, just like the rest of the world.

HECTOR.: Yeah, and if we don't try to change it to be the way we want, its going to change in ways that we won't be able to tolerate.

DORIS: Thanks for the coffee. Do me a little favor, will you?

LOLA: Don't tell my husband I came over.

DORIS: You know how slow you men are to change.

LOLA: Wouldn't change your socks, if you didn't have to.

(Crossfade to SONIA and ROSALINDA entering opposite)

SONIA: Hola, Rosalinda. ¿Como esta usted?

ROSALINDA: Very good! Keep that up and you'll be bi-lingual in no time.

SONIA: It's the least I can do. In the twenty-first century, the majority of the American population will be Hispanic.

ROSALINDA: Don't say 'Hispanic'. I hate being called something that has the word 'panic' in it.

SONIA: Oops! Guess I'm behind the curve on that one.

ROSALINDA: You are. Now we call ourselves Latinos. But that might change.

SONIA: Latinos! Cool. We're African-Americans now. But that could change at any time, too; without warning.

ROSALINDA: De veras, mi amiga.

SONIA: Yo creo que si, tambien!

DORIS: *(Coming out of house and addressing audience)* Nobody's moving anywhere, don't you see? If we do we all lose.

LOLA: We can't let our enemies win again! When we fight among ourselves, our enemies laugh!

ROSALINDA: We may sing in two different languages, but our melody is the same!

SONIA: Listen to the melody. . .

ROSALINDA: It joins us together in a deep place where long ago, our ancestors swapped recipes for living, while Europeans slumbered in caves.

SONIA: We are all mixtures. Comanche, Castilian, Ibo, Apache

LOLA: Yoruba, Hibernian, Ashkenazi, Olmec.

ROSALINDA: . . . And mixtures of mixtures!

DORIS: America is a big idea.

HECTOR: A big idea, that small people keep trying to shrink down to a size small enough to contain only themselves . . .

CARL: Leaving no room for brothers . . .

DORIS: Without any space for sisters . . .

CARL: We are all "the People."

HECTOR: We are all 'La Gente'.

ALL: We are all 'Raza.'

ROSALINDA: With, not one, but many roots . . .

LOLA: . . . Running deep into the bedrock of lost kingdoms.

ALL: We are Raza. Nueva, a new tribe for a new millenium.

DORIS: Because a people united is the greatest force in all creation.

(SONIA sings "Bridges Cross Borders" and others join in)

> Bridges-Crossing borders.
> Must be more than just a passing dream?

Bridges—Crossing over troubled waters-
Over every rocky stream

Leading to a brighter day
When neighbors will be friends.
Then, they'll lend a hand, like next of kin,
If we begin by crossing

Bridges—over borders
To journey to a world unknown-
Where sisters make room for brothers;
Young and old and almost grown

When all borders pass away,
Neighbors can be friends-
Angels up above, look down in love,
As hand in glove we're crossing . . . Bridges.

(Repeats)

THE END

Appendix A

Works by Sterling Houston

Plays

Harlem: A Renaissance Remembered, 1986
The Modernization of Sainthood, 1988
A Brief History of American Song, 1987
The Late Late Show at the Gilded Cage, 1989
Relationships: Good and Not so Good, 1989
A'lelia, 1990
Kool Jams, 1990
Travels of the Time-Train, 1990
Cheap Talk, 1992
High Yello Rose, 1992
Driving Wheel, 1992
Womandingo, 1992
Isis in Nubia, 1993
La Frontera, 1993
Miranda Rites, 1994
On the Pulse of Morning, by Maya Angelou, adapted for stage
    by Sterling Houston, 1995
Santo Negro, 1995
Black Lily and White Lily, 1996
Miss Bowden's Dream, 1998
The Alien Show: Kool Jams, 1999
Message Sent, 2000
Le Griffon, 2000
Cameoland, 20002
El Calor de Amor, 2003
Black and Blue, Four Centuries of Struggle and Transcendence, 2003
The Living Graves, 2005
The Last of the Tennessee Waltz, 2006
Leche de Luna, 2006
Millie and Christina, 2006
Hollywood and Time, 2007
Snow White and the Seven Deadly Sins, 1994
Miz Johnson and Mr. Jones, undated
The Ballad of Box Brown, undated

Novels and Novellas

Moan You Mourners (La Voz de Esperanza, 1994)

Le Griffon: : A True Tale of Supernatural Love (Pecan Grove Press, 1999)

The Secret Oral Teachings of the Sacred Walking Blues, 2005
    (unpublished)

Anthologies

Myth, Magic, and Farce: Four Multicultural Plays by Sterling Houston,
    ed. Sandra Mayo (University of North Texas Press, 2005)

Jump-Start Play Works, ed. Sterling Houston (Wings Press, 2004)

Four Plays by Sterling Houston, ed. Sandra Mayo (Urban
    Communication, Inc., 1998)

Appendix B

Awards and Recognitions

1989: *North San Antonio Times* "Gemini" Award, for the *Late Late Show at the Gilded Cage*

1990: Writing grant, City of San Antonio Department of Arts and Cultural Affairs, for *Kool Jams*

1991: Artist of the Year Award, San Antonio Business Committee for the Arts

1992: FEAT (Festival of Emerging American Theatre) Award, for *Womandingo*

1992: Artist of the Year Award, *San Antonio Light*

1992: Commission Grant, Mid-America Arts Alliance, for *La Frontera*

1992: Grant, Texas Composer's Forum, for *La Frontera*

1992: New Forms Regional Initiative Commission Grant, Rockefeller Foundation, Andy Warhol Foundation, and the National Endowment for the Arts, for *Santo Negro*

1993: Alamo Theatre Arts Council (ATAC) Globe Awards, Best Score, Best New Script, for *High Yello Rose*

1993: Grant, National Endowment for the Arts and the Andy Warhol Foundation, for *Santo Negro*

1994: Alamo Theatre Arts Council (ATAC) Globe Award, Best Original Music, for *Isis in Nubia,*

1995: Art Matters Grant, and Art Institute of Chicago's Americas Zones of Contact Series, *Santo Negro*

1995: Alamo Theatre Arts Council (ATAC) Globe Award, for *Miranda Rites*

1996: Cleveland Public Theatre Festival of New Plays Award, *Black Lily and White Lily*

1997: Citation for Contribution to Cultural Life, State of Texas, sponsored by Senator Ruth Jones McClendon

1997: Arts and Letters Award, San Antonio Public Library

1998: Commission Grant, 1998, St. Philip's College, for *Miss Bowden's Dream*

1999: Alamo Theatre Arts Council, Jasmina Wellinghoff Award for lifetime contributions to theatre

1999: Publication of Houston's *Le Griffon: a True Tale of Supernatural Love* (Pecan Grove Press)

2000: 20 Most Influential People in the Arts for the New Millenium, *San Antonio Express-News*

2001: Commission Grant, Mid-America Arts Alliance, for *La Frontera*

2001: Meet the Composer Grant, Texas Composers Forum, for *La Frontera*

2003: Grant, Rockefeller MAP (Multi-Arts Production fund), for *Cameoland*

2003: One of Ten Best Plays of the Year, S*an Antonio Express-News,* for *Cameoland*

2004: Publication of *Jump-Start PlayWorks: A Collection of Multicultural Plays and Solo Performance Works from Jump-Start Performance Co.,* edited by Sterling Houston (Wings Press)

2004: Gemini Ink, Award of Literary Excellence

Biographical Note: Sterling Houston

Sterling Houston (1945-2006), born in San Antonio, was a performer, a writer, and a prolific and innovative avant-garde playwright. During his lifetime, he wrote 33 plays, wrote three short novels, and edited anthologies. Twenty-four of his plays were first produced by Jump-Start Performance Co in San Antonio, from 1988 to 2006. Venues included the Blue Star Arts Complex (Jump-Start Theater), the Carver Cultural Center, and St. Philip's College in San Antonio. His plays were also produced in other parts of the country including New York, Cleveland, Chicago and San Francisco.

Houston worked with some of the greatest practioners of modern American theater from 1964 to 1981, including Charles Ludlum, Sam Shepard, and George C. Wolfe. Houston returned to San Antonio in 1981 and shortly afterward joined the Jump-Start Performance Co. He served as writer-in-residence and artistic director for the company from 1989 until his death in November, 2006.

Houston was known for his biting social commentary, his taste for burlesque humor, and his mastery of multiple genres. The seven plays in this collection showcase his passion for the intersection of history, myth, and folklore, and exhibit his versatile theatricality that combines domestic drama, farce, docudrama, and musical theatre and employed a variety of post-modern special effects. Ever an experimentalist, he also authored three short novels, including *Le Griffon: A True Tale of Supernatural Love* (Pecan Grove Press, 1999).

Houton's personal papers archived in the University of Texas at San Antonio's permanent San Antonio Authors Collection. A descriptive summary catalog of the collection is available at:
http://www.lib.utexas.edu/taro/utsa/00129/00129-P.html

Biographical Note: Sandra M. Mayo

Sandra M. Mayo, Ph.D., holds degrees from Syracuse University, Buffalo State, and the State University at Buffalo. She is currently the Director of Multicultural and Gender Studies and Associate Professor of Theatre at Texas State University-San Marcos. Her publications include editing and writing the introduction to *Myth, Magic, and Farce: Four Multicultural Plays by Sterling Houston,* published by the University of North Texas Press in 2005.